PAUL MILLERD

The Pathless Path

Imagining a New Story for Work and Life

This is the pathless path. Where the journey leads is to the deepest truth in you.

— Ram Dass

Contents

I

The Default Path

1

Introduction

I was extremely nervous. As the teacher of my semester-long Chinese language class called my name, my heart started to race. I took a deep breath and began. I shared the story of quitting my job, deciding to move to Taiwan, meeting the woman who would become my wife, starting an online business, and living in five different countries. It was the first time I had shared my story in another language, and as I finished, a calmness swept over my body. It was the end of a three-month period where I had felt completely alive, spending my time learning, creating, solving problems, and spending time exploring Taipei with my wife.

This would have been unimaginable to me five years earlier when I lived in New York City. I was single, spending my time at work, eating out, partying with friends, dating, and constantly plotting ways to work less or escape work altogether. I was working at a consulting firm making nearly $200,000 a year and working on projects for some of the most recognizable CEOs in the world. I was successful, and on my way to being even more successful.

This was the end result of an obsessive focus on getting ahead in my twenties. It's a state familiar to many. Study hard, get good grades, get a good job. Then put your head down and keep going, indefinitely. This is what I call the "default path."

Growing up, I thought making $100,000 a year made someone rich. When I made that amount for the first time at 27, I felt like I had more than I could ever need. Yet I opted into an identity that didn't accept such complacency. Everyone around me was always moving forward towards the next achievement.

Chasing achievements is what brought me to that New York City job working with CEOs, the final one before I decided to quit. Most mornings I came into the office and sat there struggling to start my day. I watched the people pass my desk and wondered if they felt the same stuckness as I did.

Eventually, I would start my work, helping company boards assess their senior executives to see who the next CEO of the company should be. I read through feedback reports from people throughout the company and created summarized reports of each executive's strengths and weaknesses. We like to think that once we "make it" we can finally be ourselves, but based on who the companies selected, it was clear that the longer people stay at a company, the higher odds that they would become what the company wanted. I realized I didn't want that to happen to me.

In a ten-year period, I worked for five companies and spent two years in grad school. I moved from job to job, convinced the next stop was always the final stop.

My restlessness was easy to hide because my path was filled with impressive names and achievements, and when you're on such a path, no one asks "Why are you doing this?" It took me a while to recognize this blind spot and have the courage to start asking myself those kinds of deeper questions in a serious way.

Which led me to walk away. Scratch that – run away. I even gave back a $24,000 signing bonus and missed out on a $30,000 bonus if I had been able to stick it out for another nine months. I left with the intention to become a freelance consultant, but soon enough, that story started to show its cracks as well. It didn't take me long to realize I had been on a path that wasn't mine and to find a new way forward, I would need to step into the unknown.

About a year into this journey, I stumbled upon a phrase which helped me take a deep breath. It was the idea of a "pathless path," something I found in David Whyte's book *The Three Marriages*. To Whyte, a pathless path is a paradox: "we cannot even see it is there, and we do not recognize it."[1] To me, the pathless path was a mantra to reassure myself I would be okay. After spending the first 32 years of my life always having a plan, this kind of blind trust in the universe was new, scary, and exciting. Whyte says that when we first encounter the idea of a pathless path, "we are not meant to understand what it means."

To me, however, it meant everything.

The pathless path is an alternative to the default path. It is an embrace of uncertainty and discomfort. It's a call to adventure in a world that tells us to conform. For me, it's also a gentle reminder to laugh when things feel out of control and trusting that an uncertain future is not a problem to be solved.

Ultimately, it's a new story for thinking about finding a path in life.

As the world continues to change and technology reshapes our lives, the stories we use to navigate life become outdated and come up short. People are starting to feel the disconnect between what we've been told about how the world works and what they experience. You work hard, but get laid off anyway. You have the perfect life on paper, but no time to enjoy it. You retire with millions in the bank, but no idea what to do with your time.

The pathless path has been my way to release myself from the achievement narrative that I had been unconsciously following. I was able to shift away from a life built on getting ahead and towards one focused on coming alive. I was able to grapple with the hard questions of life, the ones we try so hard to ignore. And I was able to keep moving when I realized that the hardest questions often don't have answers.

One of the biggest things the pathless path did for me was to help me reimagine my relationship with work. When I left my job, I had a narrow view of work and wanted to escape. On the pathless path, my conception expanded, and I was able to see the truth: that most people, including myself, have a deep desire to work on things that matter to them and bring forth what is inside them. It is only when we cling to the logic of the default path that we fail to see the possibilities for making that happen.

I had been following a formula for life that was supposed to guarantee happiness. It didn't. Confusion kept me on a path that wasn't mine for more than ten years. Along the way, I learned how to play the game of success and achievement, but never paused to find out what I really wanted. I found myself in rooms surrounded by business leaders and didn't quite fit in. I was in the wrong rooms, asking the wrong questions about how to live.

The Default Path

This book does not argue for or against any singular way of living, but it contests the idea that the default path is the *only* way.

By default path, I mean a series of decisions and accomplishments needed to be seen as a successful adult. These vary by country, but in the United States, we refer to this as the "American Dream," which means a life centered around a good job, owning a home, and having a family.

Researchers Dorthe Berntsen and David Rubin study what they call "life scripts," which they describe as "culturally shared expectations as to the order and timing of life events in a prototypical life course."[2] Their research found remarkable consistency across countries with regard to the events that people expect to occur in their lives. Most of these moments occur before the age of 35: graduating from school, getting a job, falling in love, and getting married.[3]

This means that for many people, expectations of life are centered around a small number of positive events that occur while we are young. Much of the rest of our lives remains unscripted and when people face inevitable setbacks, they are left without instructions on how to think or feel. While very few young people expect to have one job or career, most still rely on the logic of the default path and assume they need to have everything figured out before the age of 25. This limits the ideas of what we see as possible and many, including me, internalize the "worldly wisdom" that John Maynard Keynes once pointed out, "that it is better for reputation to fail conventionally than to succeed unconventionally."[4]

Since 2017, I've had hundreds of virtual "curiosity conversations" with people from around the world about work and life. I've seen the shame of unexpected layoffs, the panic attacks from changing jobs, and the loss of hope people experience when they can't make it work on the particular path they think they are supposed to follow. On top of that, people are ashamed to talk about these things with the people in their lives.

This anxiety is not limited to young people. Increasingly, people at the end of traditional work careers tell me they are not excited about the default story of retirement. They still have a desire to engage with the world but don't know how to make that happen. As of 2018, men and women in developed countries are expected to spend nearly 20 years in retirement.[5] As the baby boomer generation enters this new life stage, bringing with them unprecedented wealth, health, and energy, they will be looking for new stories about how to live their lives.

These stories motivate me to keep going on my own journey and give me plenty to write about. Without intending to, I've become a repository of wisdom about how to navigate life and build a better relationship with work. Much of what I've learned through these conversations has inspired this book.

Prior to embracing the pathless path, I was the friend that people came to when they had career challenges. I once worked closely with a young professional in his mid-20s who wanted to escape his current job. As he described his career options, he told me he could keep progressing at his company and become a partner or he could take a position at a client's firm and "coast," as he put it.

"Are those the only two options?" I asked. "Yes," he replied. I listed a few other paths that he conceded were possible, but he added, "I don't know anyone who has done that." Many people fall into this trap. We are convinced that the only way forward is the path we've been on or what we've seen people like us do. This is a silent conspiracy that constrains the possibilities of our lives.

I was testing out a side gig as a career coach when I first met that young professional. He hated his job and wanted to make a change. As he found a new role, working in another company, he lost all motivation to keep working with me and exploring the things that mattered to him.

This disappointed me. I wanted him to see the potential I saw. Yet in my own life, I was doing the same thing. With every new job, I convinced myself I was thriving. But what I was really doing was trying to escape feeling stuck.

I was too afraid to have a deeper conversation with myself. The kind that might pull me towards a different kind of life.

Why This Matters

For most of my life, I've had the gift of seeing the greatness in others. It hurts when I see people stuck or unable to pursue their dreams, and I want to do anything I can to help them. In writing this book, I realized that this has everything to do with my parents.

I won the childhood lottery. I had two parents that devoted their lives to creating the best life possible for my siblings and me. They did this by figuring out what they were best at and then giving it their complete commitment.

For my mother, it was being an active parent. Right from the start, she had an intuitive sense of my needs. She gave me space to make my own decisions and I learned how to take ownership of my life. She helped remove any obstacles in my way and helped me grow into a confident adult. At every step of my journey, the courage to take the next step was a direct result of her abundant love and compassion.

My father prioritized work. I struggled with this for many years. I wished he was around more. As I got older, however, I realized that this decision was just as hard on him and that he didn't have any other choice.

At 19 he took a job at a manufacturing company and didn't think about working anywhere else for another 41 years. The story he told himself throughout his entire career was that he had to work harder than everyone else. Why? He didn't have a degree. As he earned promotions, he found himself surrounded by people with impressive credentials and likely felt more pressure to keep up. Yet he never complained. He woke up every day at 5 a.m., put in 12-hour days, said yes to every single thing asked of him, and in doing so, was able to have a remarkable career and ensured that my siblings and I had more options than he did.

My mother also believed that not having a degree held her back and she was right. A couple of years after college, I helped her apply for a job at another school as a director of a financial aid department. The recruiting committee said that her cover letter "was one of the best they had seen" and that she was the best candidate, but because she didn't have a degree, they were offering the position to someone else.

This hurt me so much. I knew that my mother was smart and capable and that a degree had nothing to do with what she had to offer the world.

The best option available for my parents was the default path. This worked remarkably well for them, which is what made leaving it so damn hard. I know how much they sacrificed so that I would have better career opportunities. However, what they really gave me was so much more than the ability to succeed in school and work. It was space to dream, take risks, and be able to explore more possibilities for my life.

Many people find it difficult to create change in their lives because they lack someone that believes in them. I have parents, aunts, uncles, grandparents, teachers, and managers who believe in me. Their support gives me an advantage and because of this, nothing motivates me more than trying to be that person for others. I am inspired by what the writer Leo Rosten once argued was the purpose of life: "to be useful, to be honorable, to be compassionate, to have it make some difference that you have lived and lived well."[6] The pathless path has helped me see that quitting my job was never about escaping work or living an easier life, it was about using the gifts I received from my parents to benefit others.

Helping people live courageously so that they can thrive is one of the most important things in the world. I want to see people live the lives they are capable of, not just the ones they think they are allowed to live.

I wrote this book to show you that this is possible.

My journey on the pathless path is about slowly figuring this out and helping countless people from around the world realize the same thing.

Now it's your turn. What follows is not a simple playbook, but an invitation to join me on the pathless path to see what might happen if we imagine a new story together.

Ready?

2

Getting Ahead

The ease of having an ambition is that it can be explained to others; the very disease of ambition is that it can be so easily explained to others. – David Whyte

World Class Hoop-Jumper

The term "hoop-jumper" was coined by writer and former professor William Deresiewicz to describe the behavior of his students at Yale, who seemed more concerned about getting A's and adding bullet points to their resumes than using their time at one of the world's best universities to follow their curiosity.[7]

Focused on landing good internships or jobs, or getting accepted into graduate schools, his students based their choices on which classes and activities would improve their chances. Many had been playing this game for their entire lives, moving from one elite school to the next, fueled by lofty parental expectations.

Even though I ended up playing the same games, my childhood was remarkable for its lack of pressure, hands-off parents, and a genuine love of school. In high school, I was a top student but never considered applying to top-ranked schools. I was only interested in going to the University of Connecticut, my home-state school. The biggest reason? I could get five-dollar tickets to sit in the student section of the men's basketball games.

When I was accepted, I was admitted into the honors program, and assigned to live in a building with other honors students. I didn't know it at the time, but this would have an enormous impact on my future. I was surrounded by people with bold aspirations and impressive achievements. People with perfect SAT scores, full scholarships, and five-year plans. I was genuinely surprised to hear about the extensive processes that some students had gone through to pick a school, weighing the trade-offs among scholarships, rankings, job opportunities, and access to grad schools. I just wanted to go to basketball games.

But these people became my friends and I started to want what they wanted. They embodied a *success ethic* that focused on maximizing achievements in the present to create better options in the future. I started to resent the high school I had attended, where the guidance counselor suggested I try a major other than engineering because "it was hard." *Why hadn't people pushed me harder? Should I have applied to better schools?*

As a late arrival to this game, I didn't have the baggage of anxiety and stress that a lot of my new friends seemed to have after years of chasing achievements. I was shocked at how some of them worked to exhaustion, filling their schedules beyond what they could handle. I wasn't willing to compete on that level, but I still wanted to keep up, so I became obsessed with figuring out the rules and learning how to hack the system.

During my first semester of college, I created an Excel spreadsheet of my schedule for the next four years. Then I cross-referenced it with a site called RateMyProfessor.com so I could optimize my schedule based on the easiest graders for my courses. In my second year, I figured out how to petition the school to take more than the maximum 18 credits so that I could add easy classes, or as we called them, "guaranteed A's," to my course load.

When I started college, earning an A was table stakes for my honors classmates and me. This was the result of decades of grade inflation. By the mid-2000s, 42% of college students received A's in their classes.[8] This was a shift from the past. In the 1960s, earning an A was the third most likely grade after C's and a B's. For us, since getting an A was not only possible but expected, my classmates and I spent as much time finding loopholes to improve our grades as we did studying for tests.

I loved finding the loopholes. My dual engineering and business degree was challenging, but it conveniently avoided the hardest engineering classes. I also took classes at weird times to get easy grading professors. I still pursued impressive achievements like graduating with honors, but I picked a thesis advisor and classes that wouldn't push me too hard. With every internship offer, Dean's list award, and scholarship I earned, the intoxicating feeling of success ran through my body. I felt like I had it all figured out.

I was becoming a hoop-jumper just like Deresiewicz's students at Yale, internalizing the idea that education is "doing your homework, getting the answers, acing the test." I had not developed a sense that "something larger is at stake" as Deresiewicz says, and only was playing the game of student, not using my mind. [9]

Strategy Consulting

By the end of my junior year, I had a high GPA, completed multiple internships, and had won several awards. Yet as I entered senior year, I was about to commit to the first goal worthy of my hoop-jumping ambitions. I decided to attempt to break into the elite world of strategy consulting.

Strategy consulting was born out of the growth of the manufacturing industry in the late 1800s in the United States. Originally referred to as "consulting engineers," people like Frederick Taylor, Arthur D. Little, and Edwin Booz worked with manufacturing plants to increase their efficiency and profitability.[10] They eventually helped establish some of the first consulting firms and throughout the 20th century, these companies evolved and expanded in scope and ambition. By the time I graduated, it was a multi-billion-dollar industry with hundreds of firms spanning the globe. These firms worked with CEOs and senior executives on large, important problems. For young ambitious people, they offered the potential to skip "climbing the ladder" and work directly on the most interesting business problems immediately after graduation.

Initially, these companies only hired from elite schools like Harvard and Yale. Later, as the industry expanded, they recruited more widely but were still selective. The University of Connecticut was not one of them, and instead was what they called a "non-target" school. I knew it would be a challenge to break into the industry, but I still wanted to give it a shot.

Committing to this goal gave me a mission, which also helped me ignore the growing anxiety about the transition from school to the "real world." I had no wisdom to draw upon for navigating this important phase in life other than what everyone around me was doing: picking a path.

The modern world offers an abundance of paths. In one sense this is great. It's the result of an industrial system and resulting prosperity that has created opportunities for people around the world. However, the proliferation of paths presents a challenge. With so many options it can be tempting to pick a path that offers certainty rather than doing the harder work of figuring out what we really want.

A friend, Ranjit Saimbi, who has since left law to pursue software development, shared that he was attracted to the law profession because "the steps are laid out for you." A career in the law signaled to others that he "was a serious and intelligent person." But the longer he spent on the path, he realized that the real promise had been that "life's existential fears are traded for certainty."[11]

The paths that Ranjit and I were drawn to also offered something else: prestige. Though hard to define, prestige can be thought of as the attention you get when you do things that others see as impressive. Paul Graham, the founder of a startup incubator and mentor to thousands of young people, sees this attention as a trap. In his view, prestige is "a powerful magnet that warps even your beliefs about what you enjoy."[12]

Ranjit and I were both pulled by the force of the impressive stories associated with prestigious jobs like strategy consulting and law. These paths are too good to be true for driven young people who want to turn their success in school into something tangible for others to see. Zen philosopher Alan Watts argued that "the desire for security and the feeling of insecurity are the same thing," and that "we look for this security by fortifying and enclosing ourselves in innumerable ways. We want the protection of being 'exclusive' and 'special.'"[13] This was exactly what I was looking for.

Entering my senior year of college, the pull of prestige took the wheel and I started plotting ways to overcome my status as a "non-target" applicant.

Chasing Prestige

What I really wanted was to be part of the "inner ring," which C.S. Lewis famously detailed in a lecture given at King's College in 1944. He argued, "...in all men's lives at certain periods...one of the most dominant elements is the desire to be inside the local Ring and the terror of being left outside."[14]

Before the fall semester of senior year, I had built a spreadsheet of consulting companies and other jobs perceived as prestigious. This was the inner ring I cared about. Beyond consulting companies, it included investment banks, technology startups, and hedge funds. I wasn't picky about the type of work I'd be doing, I just wanted it to be seen as impressive. I spent most of that semester in a frenzy, searching for companies I had missed, networking, sending cold e-mails, and trying to land interviews. Unfortunately, most of my efforts were met with near-instant rejection. My credentials were good enough but most of the companies had met their hiring targets with students from better schools.

Out of a couple of hundred companies, I did have a handful of interviews. This gave me a peek into the secret world of the inner ring. One of these interviews brought me to North Carolina where I took part in a "superday" for Wachovia's investment bank. A superday is a two-day ordeal that includes meals, casual conversations with employees and other interviewees, and finally, several formal interviews on the second day.

When I arrived, I checked into my hotel and made my way to a high-end cocktail bar down the street. Within fifteen minutes, I discovered that in a group of 30–40 people I was one of the few "non-target" applicants. Realizing this, I started to feel like I had crashed a wedding. Some of the candidates mentioned that their friends from school were already working at the company or that Wachovia was "only" a backup option. They were intrigued that I had landed an interview, but ultimately did not see me as a threat. These students from places like the University of Virginia, Duke, and Cornell oozed confidence, and as I now realize, they were already part of the inner ring. All they had to do now was figure out which company badge they would be wearing come graduation.

The next day, I went through the motions in eight 30-minute inter-views, but the entire time it felt like both the interviewers and I already knew what would happen. I received the rejection call two days later, and by the end of the semester, every company on my list had either rejected or ignored my application.

Still, my first close look inside the inner ring, while awkward, furthered my motivation. Now I wanted not only to break into this exclusive world but also to rid myself of the shame I felt that weekend, the feeling that I was not good enough.

Despite not breaking into the inner ring, I had still been working on a backup plan, which was to work in one of General Electric's (GE) leadership development programs. At the time, GE still had a great reputation in the business world and prided itself on shying away from hiring the elite students I had been competing against. They preferred to hire people just like me, high achievers at big public schools.

I had interned at GE prior to my senior year and had the option to return the following year in an engineering role. However, during that summer, when I was first infected with the desire to chase prestige, I found out about their Financial Management Program. It was the inner ring within GE and seen as the fast track to success inside the company. Even though my internship had been in engineering, and I had taken only a few finance classes, I applied to the program and convinced recruiters that this was my ideal path. When I got the offer, I canceled the other interviews I had on-campus. GE wasn't part of the inner ring I cared about, but it was still seen as one of the best jobs you could get at my school.

Why would anyone go through the trouble of applying to so many jobs? One part of the answer is that I have always enjoyed the job search process. The more complicated and more accurate answer would be that I got sucked into a chase after achievement in an environment where maximizing potential success was one of the best things to do with your time. My friends all had impressive plans after graduation, and I didn't want to be left behind. People were impressed by the job I was taking at GE, and I liked how the attention made me feel. I felt smart. It didn't matter that I had never worked in finance and had never spent any time in Ohio or the Midwest, where I would be located. Out of all the jobs I could get from my school, this was one of the best and the magnet of prestige convinced me that was what I wanted.

After graduation, I made the two-day drive to Ohio with my cousin Brian. I remember two things about the drive: *Hey There, Delilah* coming on the radio every forty minutes and being filled with a sense of unease. For the first time, I would be living outside of a 15-mile bubble in Connecticut. Moving to a new city and working for a great company like GE was exciting, but deep down I felt like I wasn't where I wanted to be. I tried to pretend I was happy to be starting the job, but I wanted more.

My unease quickly morphed into a desire to escape. When I joined, GE was a 100-year-old company with a great reputation but was starting to show its age. I couldn't imagine spending the rest of my career there, let alone two years. No one seemed to care about anything. My colleagues had been coming to the same desks for decades and were more interested in their retirement portfolios than working and told me that if not for the benefits, they probably wouldn't show up.

My program included four 6-month rotations in different parts of the business, and I barely finished two. I decided I was going to quit as I drove to Jacksonville, Florida, for my second rotation. I called my friend Mike, who was set to move to Boston for a job later that year. "Mike, if I move to Boston in June, do you want to live together?" "Hell yeah!" he said. It was settled. Boston was a place where I might have a better shot at landing a job at one of those companies in the inner ring while being closer to my friends and family.

In Jacksonville, I ramped up part two of my job search, applying to many of the same companies that had rejected me only a year earlier. Crazily enough, this period ended with me landing my dream job. Yes, that's right. About a month after arriving in Florida, I found a job posting for a research analyst at McKinsey & Company, the company at the top of my list. After several rounds of interviews, I landed an offer to join the company in the Boston office.

It felt too good to be true, and how people perceived this achievement differed from how I experienced it. Others saw an impressive new job at McKinsey, a smart career move. Yet for me it was a lucky outcome after a year of restlessness, immaturity, insecurity, and a desperate desire to escape.

Part of me had been secretly excited about quitting my job and moving to a new city without a job, drawn by the possibilities of adventure. That part of me would get its chance but it would have to wait several years.

I said goodbye to Florida and drove a U-Haul back north with my father, excited about my next step. I had a second chance at starting my post-college life, this time in the real inner ring.

The Inner Ring

Walking into the office on that first day, I was thrilled. At McKinsey, I was grateful to be surrounded by enthusiastic and curious people instead of people working for the weekend. I worked with managers that cared about me and pushed me to improve.

Although I felt like an outsider that had somehow broken into an exclusive world, I slowly started to absorb the norms and desires of the people around me. Unlike at GE, where mentioning any interests beyond the job was taboo, at McKinsey people openly shared their ambitions to attend top graduate schools, become CEOs, or work for other prestigious institutions. For many of my coworkers, McKinsey was only a stop on the way to bigger things.

I adopted this attitude and embraced a version of a career which philosopher Andrew Taggart, who writes about our modern relationship to work, describes as "a first-person work-centric story of progress about an individual's life course."[15] From this perspective, my career was not a series of jobs, but a high-stakes proposition, one where falling behind felt like failure. My colleagues and I dealt with this pressure by constantly talking about potential career paths and "exit options." This was helpful for someone new to this world like me. I could figure out how to stay in the inner ring by following the wisdom of my peers.

A year went by and I decided my next step was going to a top business school. This idea did not emerge out of thin air. Talks of applications, essays, and school rankings filled the daily lunchroom conversations. These people were my friends and when they were accepted into elite business schools like Harvard and Stanford, it seemed obvious that I should do the same thing. This is the trap of prestigious career paths. Instead of thinking about what you want to do with your life, you default to the options most admired by your peers.

In describing the power of the inner ring, C.S. Lewis warns that, "unless you take measures to prevent it, this desire is going to be one of the chief motives of your life, from the first day on which you enter your profession until the day when you are too old to care." He believed "any other kind of life, if you lead it, will be the result of conscious and continuous effort."

In this world, the natural thing was to leave McKinsey, despite loving the work, because that was what everyone did. Near the end of my second year, I was accepted into a dual-degree program at the

Massachusetts Institute of Technology. If you had shown me Lewis' quote and tried to convince me there was any "other kind of life" I would not have believed it.

The path I was on was too good to be true and I was more than happy to be on it.

Existential Opening

The philosopher Andrew Taggart believes that crisis moments lead to "existential openings" that force us to grapple with the deepest questions about life.[16]

He argues there are two typical ways this happens. One is the "way of loss," when things that matter are taken from us, such as loved ones, our health, or a job. The other path is the "way of wonderment," when we are faced with moments of undeniable awe and inspiration.

I first experienced the "way of loss" in 2010 at the end of my second year at McKinsey, a month before starting graduate school.

I was at my parent's house and we received a call from my sister who was visiting my grandfather. She seemed worried. My grandfather had been diagnosed with pancreatic cancer. He had dealt with health issues for years, but this felt different. As soon as I heard, I had a lump in my throat. I sat on the back deck with my mother trying to make sense of the news.

We did what almost everyone does when faced with a harsh truth: we denied it. It was early May and my grandparents were scheduled to return to Connecticut for the summer in a few weeks. The news was bad, but neither my mother nor I thought it was urgent. He'd make it back to Connecticut we told ourselves.

Life had other plans. By mid-week, he had taken a turn for the worse, and by Friday, almost all of my relatives from across the country had boarded planes to see him in Arizona. I arrived towards the end of the week and shared the back seat with my cousins as my uncle drove us to my grandfather's house. That 30-minute ride was one of the longest in my life. No one spoke and we were all thinking the same thing: *please still be alive.*

Over the next couple of days, 25 of us were scattered around the two-bedroom house taking turns visiting him one-on-one and as a family. I remember standing around the bed holding hands with my family and feeling the deepest pain of my life as tears streamed down my cheeks.

My grandfather was a larger-than-life figure, and I loved spending time with him. When I was 13, he bought a house on the lake in my town, and I developed a deeper relationship with him and my grandmother. The house became not only a second home, but a gathering space for friends, family, and acquaintances. The door was open to everyone as long as they agreed to eat my grandfather's food.

He never talked about his childhood, but according to his siblings, after their mother died, he was sent to live on a farm with his uncle. Sometime around fourth grade, he stopped going to school so that he could start working with his uncle. He didn't have a childhood filled with love and support. He chose to deal with it by trying to do better for his children and grandchildren and he succeeded. Like many of my cousins, we feel like we won the lottery growing up with a family like ours, where thanks to my grandfather we had access to a magical world filled with love, laughter, and possibility.

Sitting in the house in Arizona, I knew I was about to lose him, one of the most important people in my life. Those few days were filled with tears and overwhelming emotion, but also with beauty and a profound sense of meaning. The proof of his life's work was in front of us. He had succeeded in creating a world better than the one he had grown up in. It was clear to me in those moments that family, love, and relationships were the most important things in the world.

Despite this clarity, I struggled to remain present in the days before he passed. I couldn't stop thinking about work. What if my colleagues needed me? To settle my anxiety, I drove to a local café and checked my email. Everything was fine. A colleague messaged me, "What are you doing!? Go back with your family, we got you!" I smiled and closed my laptop.

Driving back from the café, I was angry at myself. Why had I been so worried about work, something that was clearly not important? As I walked back into my grandfather's house, the house was silent. He was taking his final breaths. Had I nearly missed this moment because of some silly emails? I joined hands with my family, said a prayer, and left my worries aside for the next few days.

That experience sent me down the "way of loss," opening me up to the questions I had ignored by orienting my life around my work.

What was I living for?

What did I really want?

How did I want to look back on my life when it was my time to go?

Difficult questions but ones that I was finally ready to contemplate.

Business School

I started business school a month after losing my grandfather. I was excited to be in school again, but his loss overshadowed everything and opened me up emotionally. In those months, everything was filled with meaning. Relationships felt more important. Books, songs, and movies made me cry, and I became more curious about everything.

I tried to integrate these changes into my life by shifting my attention away from my career and towards my friendships, relationships, and learning. I prioritized classes that interested me, and I didn't pay as much attention to grades. In my first semester, one of my classes was filled with what I determined was pointless busy-work. I decided to skip most of the assignments, earning a C+ in the class, the first "C" of my life, and a failing grade in business school.

I still passed most of my classes, but after three years of putting my career first, I was able to put life first. My memories of business school are the conversations with friends at Beacon Hill Pub, watching Jersey Shore at Mike's, cultural celebrations, formal parties, intramural hockey, and basketball games, touring factories across the world, and most notably, performing an Irish Jig in front of 500 people. In a class at the end of the two years, my friend Kurtis shared that he thought I was someone that "lived life to its fullest." This was surprising and humbling to hear. It was the first time I realized that I had leaned into the questions that arose after losing my grandfather and had focused more on creating memories than getting good grades.

Unfortunately, I wasn't on a permanent vacation. I spent all my savings and took $70,000 in debt with an intention to continue on my path.

McKinsey had a program that would pay for school if you committed to returning to work there for at least two years. I was so confident that I didn't want to return to consulting that I never considered it. Unfortunately, by the time recruiting started in the second year, I had not come up with any other plan. So I applied to all the same consulting firms that I had in college.

The companies were confused. McKinsey was seen as the top firm, so why was I applying to their competitors? My explanations didn't suffice, and all of the big firms rejected me. Then McKinsey rejected me too. I had been far too casual about the whole process and assumed that they would accept me. This was naïve. I was walking down Charles Street in Boston when I got the call. It was embarrassing. I felt like a loser. I might be the only person ever rejected by a company both before *and* after having worked there. Was I back to where I had been just a few years earlier, still trying to break into the inner ring?

Now, it's easy to see that I wasn't as committed to this path as my classmates and when I was "putting my life first" they were preparing for interviews.

Cracks in my career identity were starting to appear, but I was barely aware of them and had no conception of any other kind of life other than the default path I was on.

Months after most of my classmates had secured offers, a small consulting firm in Boston offered me a position. The opportunity was exciting, but it enabled me to ignore those emerging cracks. I had loosened my attachment to "Paul as a successful person," but was still firmly located in that successful world.

Health Crisis

The most interesting thing about the company I joined was the part-time consultants we hired to augment our projects, giving me exposure to the emerging gig economy. In addition to normal consulting projects, we recruited and staffed these consultants on short-term projects. These people, self-described "independent consultants," were fascinating. Everyone had a unique story and way of working. Some worked three days per week. Others worked for six months and then took six months off to travel. Some people worked on side projects and others spent time with their families. This was the first time I had direct contact with anyone who did anything other than work full-time. I was intrigued.

I might have explored that kind of life sooner if I had not spent most of my 18 months at the company dealing with health issues. In my first weeks at the company, I developed a cold that never went away. Persistent fatigue took over my body and over a couple of months, I also started experiencing bouts of brain fog and physical pain throughout my body. My life became a blur. I went through the motions at work and spent the rest of my time going from doctor to doctor trying to figure out what was wrong.

I developed strategies to deal with exhaustion and pain and blocked off at least 10-12 hours every night for sleep. Somehow, I still showed up every day and did as well as I could. About five months after the issues began, I was working on a client project in Princeton, New Jersey, when the doctor called with what I thought was good news. Tests confirmed I had a complex case of Lyme disease and there was a treatment she thought could help.

I started taking the medicine and immediately found myself in more pain. Doctors call this a "herx" reaction, something that occurs from the die-off of a bacterial infection, common for people dealing with Lyme disease. I spent eight hours at the client's office building an impressive spreadsheet, drenched in sweat, trying to handle the pain. I couldn't wait to get back to my hotel room.

That room might have been impressive in 1980, but by 2012 it existed only to house corporate types like me doing business somewhere along Route 1, a road lined with office parks, chain restaurants, and hotels. Randomly, the room had a large jacuzzi bathtub in the middle of the bedroom and I decided to use it to relieve my discomfort. As I sat in the tub, surrounded by the room's off-brown wallpaper, I felt helpless and afraid.

I made it through the week and that weekend I called Peter, the head of our office, and told him everything. He clearly understood how scared I was because when I proposed taking a week off or working remotely, he suggested I take a month off, paid, to focus on recovery. I was worried about letting him and the client down, but he told me that those things were trivial. At the time, our firm was struggling and as the head of the office, he put his own job at stake by pausing an important client project. It was a moment of leadership that inspired me.

Unfortunately, I didn't improve. One month became several and I went from paid to unpaid leave. Several treatments seemed to work before becoming ineffective. My doctor was just as confused, and I drifted into despair. Why me? When would this nightmare end?

To process these questions, I wrote. I had written the occasional blog post over the years, but this was the first time writing became necessary. I was a typical guy who hid his emotions and writing gave me a way to share without dealing with the discomfort of doing so in person. I created a blog called "Lyme Sucks" to share my progress with concerned friends and family. Over time, writing the blog became an essential part of maintaining hope. It wasn't easy, and the following post shows how desperate I was for good news:

January 8th, 2013 - *I've written a couple blog posts over the past couple months that I never posted because I deemed them too depressing or emotional. I decided to go ahead with this one because I threw some fun stuff in at the end. If anything, it will give you some insight into what people go through when they get sick. A lot of what I struggle with is really irrational and wouldn't ever occur to me if I was healthy, but I am learning more every day how to cope with it all. I was ignorant of people suffering before I got sick last year, and I've definitely learned a lot. Hopefully I can be there for others in the future that are going through tough things in their life.*

For me, these blog posts are a good way to vent and figure out my own thoughts. Generally, I am in good spirits and happy, but every new day is tough to get through. I can't even really describe the panic that comes over me during moments of doubt and fear, but I've realized those are part of the journey. When I come up for air, I realize how great things are, how lucky I am and that things aren't so bad. I appreciate the friends and family that stick by me when things get ugly. I need all of your help to keep the good times rolling and helping me through those bad moments.

By forcing my fingers to type sentences filled with optimism and hope, I was able to keep that part of me alive. This is the hardest thing about being sick. It isn't like a breakup when people tell you it will get better and you know they're right. When you're sick, you have to believe you will get better even though your body is telling you you're crazy to think that.

My version of "better" was to restart my career. I could start working again, hang out with my friends, do the things I liked, and pretend that nothing had ever happened. I shared this desire with my friend Jordan over pizza: "Just wait until I recover, then you can get to know how fun I really am." His reply shocked me: "Paul, that's crazy, I've only known you since you've been sick and you're still pretty great." I tried to change his mind, but I couldn't.

The truth was that my experience of the illness was changing me and there would be no going back. Jordan's compassion gave me the courage to abandon my attachment to seeing myself as a "broken" sick person waiting to restart my life and realize that something new was likely emerging.

With a new doctor in Boston, I found better treatments that worked and after more than a year of struggling, I started to improve. I returned to work part-time and eventually full-time, but I was not the same person. While I was sick, I had contemplated the question, "what would people think if I couldn't work again?" and had been surprised by my answer.

I would be okay. So much of my identity had been connected with being a high achiever. Straight A's. Dean's List. McKinsey. MIT. When I was sick, I would have traded every last credential for a single day of feeling okay.

As I started to feel better, a different kind of energy showed up in my life. Professors Richard Tedeschi and Lawrence Calhoun have suggested that many people who face crises often experience "post-traumatic growth" and that this manifests as an "appreciation for life in general, more meaningful interpersonal relationships, an increased sense of personal strength, changed priorities, and a richer existential and spiritual life."[17]

This is exactly what I experienced over the next few years. Through a series of unexpected steps, I was shifting towards embracing the pathless path.

3

Work, Work, Work

Until I had to take a leave from my job during my health crisis, work had been a fact of life for me. I, like many others, had expected to work in a full-time job for most of my adult life. My illness helped me see the fragility of this worldview because now I understood that building a life around work was not so simple.

My new perspective on work led me down a deep rabbit hole of questions and curiosities that led to me leaving my path and also led to this book. This is why before we move forward in my story, we need to take a step back.

If we are going to imagine a new way forward for our work and our lives, we need to understand where our current ideas from work come from and how they have changed.

Where Do Work Beliefs Come From?

German historian Max Weber found that the "spirit of capitalism" struggled to take hold in societies that embraced a "traditionalist" mindset towards work.[18] In Weber's view, a "traditionalist" view of work is one where people work as much as they need to maintain their current lifestyle, and once that aim is achieved, they stop working.

In my travels, I have been surprised to find this perspective alive and well all over the world. In Mexico, I overheard a conversation about hiring locals: "You can't pay people too much because they'll stop working!" The idea that people might decide to work less is hard for some people to imagine. This person, a foreigner, likely grew up in a culture like mine where working in a formal job continuously throughout adulthood is what most people do.

The difference between working to meet one's needs versus meeting expectations raises a question. When did this shift occur and why did it not happen universally?

It might surprise you that in Greece, during the time of Aristotle more than 2,000 years ago, work was simply considered a necessary evil. The prime aim of life according to philosophers was "Eudaimonia," which translates literally as "happiness," but is better expressed as "flourishing." In Aristotle's words, "the more contemplation, the more happiness there is in a life." Contemplating one's place in the universe was seen as one of the most worthwhile things to do and at minimum, more important than the "money-making life," which Aristotle described as "something quite contrary to nature...for it is merely useful as a means to something else."[19]

For the next 1,500 years, most of the world either remained skeptical of work or saw it simply as a way to meet basic needs. The latter idea was strengthened by the Catholic conception of work.

Genesis, the first book of the Christian Old Testament, mentions work as God is condemning Adam for eating fruit from the Tree of Life. God tells him that only "through painful toil" will Adam continue to eat fruit and only "by the sweat of your brow will you eat your food until you return to the ground." Later, in the New Testament, St. Paul warns against idleness more directly: "He who shall not work shall not eat." In regard to those who refuse, he continues: "do not associate with them, in order that they may feel ashamed."[20]

The lesson is clear: work is a duty. However, it was still in a limited sense. We see this articulated by 13th-century Catholic priest Thomas Aquinas, as he argues "labor is only necessary 'naturali ratione' [by natural reason] for the maintenance of individual and community."[21] People should be expected to work, but the reason is to meet the needs of our families and communities.

In the 1500s, Martin Luther and John Calvin expanded this definition as part of what is now known as the Protestant Reformation. They had grown disappointed in religious leaders and attacked them for living idly in monasteries. Their angle of attack was one's relationship to work. Max Weber summarizes the shift, saying that the way to honor God, "was not to surpass worldly morality in monastic asceticism, but solely through the fulfillment of the obligations imposed upon the individual by his position in the world. That was his calling."[22]

With the introduction of a "calling," Luther and then Calvin both wanted to undermine the authority of the Catholic Church to govern an individual's relationship with God. Luther took issue with the Church's system of "indulgences," in which people paid the Church to absolve them of their sins. He thought individuals should be able to have their own relationship with God. Calvin paired Luther's increase in individual freedom with the idea that everyone is predestined to serve God through a specific calling. Working hard in the area of one's calling determines the status of a person's relationship with God.

In the 1940s, philosopher Erich Fromm summarized this transformation, saying, "in the Northern European countries, from the 16th century on, man developed an obsessional craving to work which had been lacking in a free man before that period." [23] Following the Reformation, then, work as an end in itself was no longer a crazy idea. People traded one master, the Catholic Church, for another, their vocation. But along with greater freedom and self-determination came the anxiety and insecurity of never really knowing if you were working hard enough or doing the right thing. The Church's expectations had always provided a way to measure "goodness," and for many, these benchmarks no longer applied.

Over the last 500 years, this freedom has taken us in many different directions, yet remnants of the Catholic and Protestant conceptions of work are still with us. When entrepreneur Gary Vaynerchuk tells us in his book *Crush It* to "wake up before everybody else and work into the night. Hustle," he accepts both the duty of work and absolute commitment to work as integral to life.[24] Oprah Winfrey channels a modern spin on Calvin's calling, arguing that "each of us has a personal calling." To her, the "best way to succeed is to discover what you love and then find a way to offer it to others in the form of service, working hard, and also allowing the energy of the universe to lead you."[25]

These Catholic and Protestant perspectives on work are deeply embedded in the modern default path view of work that spans the globe but has become detached from the time periods and traditions from which they emerged. Religious scholars point out that the Protestant "work ethic" is more than a blind obsession with work. It is paired with thrift, self-discipline, and humility. Yet as fewer people look to religion for wisdom on how to navigate life, they are only left with the watered-down version of these views.

In Anne Helen Peterson's widely read essay "How Millennials Became the Burnout Generation," she voiced her confusion with work as she wrote that she had "...internalized the idea that I should be working all the time. Why have I internalized that idea? Because everything and everyone in my life has reinforced it – explicitly and implicitly – since I was young."[26]

Peterson's experience is similar to my own. As I was growing up, work was such an obvious goal of life that I never paused for a moment to question it. Adults talked about work all the time and constantly asked me what I wanted to do when I grew up. Schools reinforced this perspective and we learned to study hard to earn good grades to get a good job. As I grew older, I was convinced that a good career was the most important thing in life. Later, I was shocked to learn that for most of human history, this was not the case.

It Was an Anomaly!

The educated, hardworking masses are still doing what they're told, but they're no longer getting what they deserve. – Seth Godin

The modern version of the default path was born after World War II, in a period of unprecedented economic growth. This shift in thinking was led by the United States which, due to its financial and industrial advantages, achieved a period of success now known as the "long boom" during which annual GDP growth rates of at least four to five percent were the norm.

This economy generated full-time jobs with good incomes, benefits, and career opportunities, enabling a broad middle class to reach new levels of wealth and material comfort. Professor Raj Chetty at Harvard found that nine out of ten people born right after World War II did better economically than their parents.[27] Over time people came to expect constant advancement in their lives. John Steinbeck captured the sentiment in his book *America and Americans* in 1966:

> *No longer was it even acceptable that the child should be like his parents and live as they did; he must be better, live better, know more, dress more richly, and if possible, change from father's trade to a profession. This dream became touchingly national.*[28]

The baby boomer generation was born in the middle of this period, came of age at the tail end of it, and rose to leadership in global institutions by the end of the 20th century. By the time I graduated from college in 2007, the idea that life should be built around a good corporate job was so sacred that almost everyone had forgotten that only 100 years earlier most people worked on farms.

Peter Thiel, born right after the baby boom generation, reflected on this mentality in his book *Zero to One*, saying, "Since tracked careers worked for them [the baby boomers], they can't imagine that they won't work for their kids, too."[29]

Asset manager, writer, and baby boomer Jim O'Shaughnessy argues that this approach to life is flawed and his generation's mistake was to assume that the paths that worked for them would work forever:

> *We made a mistake and by that, I mean my generation and my parents' generation. The mistake we made was thinking that the period from 1946 to 1980 was the norm. No, it was not!* **It was the anomaly!** *We had just wiped out the manufacturing capabilities of anyone who could challenge us. So, the idea that you had that job with the gold watch, and you could work there for your entire career and raise a family of four and all of that, that was an anomaly.*[30]

During that stretch of time, it would have been a mistake to opt-out of the default path because as Thiel points out, "whether you were born in 1945 or 1950 or 1955, things got better every year for the first 18 years of your life, and it had nothing to do with you."[31]

By the time I graduated from college many decades later, I assumed that the path to a good life was through a steady career path at a big company. Now I know that what I assumed was an outcome of a certain way of working was instead accidental meaning. The paths that enabled people to thrive were the result of unique economic and historical circumstances and as I entered the workforce, these circumstances were no longer.

A look at the company where my father worked for 41 years demonstrates this point. During the first 20 years of his career, in the 1980s and 1990s, the company's sales grew on average by more than 14 percent per year. Over the next 21 years, the growth rate slowed to a little more than four percent per year. My father hadn't joined a big, boring company when he was young; instead, he joined a rocket ship, something closer to the fast-growing tech startups of the 2000s.

It wasn't until my early 30s that I started to suspect something was amiss. Like many of the people I knew, I was single, renting, and living and working in a city away from my hometown. Those who were starting families were overwhelmed with the costs of daycare, healthcare, and housing. We entered adulthood thinking we could copy-and-paste what our parents had done, but it was more complicated than that. Factors that support meaningful lives, like economic growth across all sectors, a young population, two-parent households, generous pensions, and company loyalty were anomalies of the past, as O'Shaughnessy points out.

Starting my career, I didn't understand any of this. Plus, I was too busy getting sucked into a new idea. That you didn't simply work to live, but that it should be one of the most important things in your life.

The Meaningful Work Trap

My generation entered the workforce with high expectations. We didn't want to see work merely as an obligation, we also wanted it to be meaningful and fulfilling. We wanted the modern version of the "calling" that Oprah talked about.

This idea gained popularity in the late 1990s. In "Jobs, Careers, and Callings," a famous study by Yale professor Amy Wrzesniewski and others, people were asked if they defined their work as a job, career, or a calling. People who defined their work as a calling saw their work as "inseparable from their life" and worked, "not for financial gain or career advancement, but instead for the fulfillment that doing the work brings to the individual." The researchers boldly concluded that if people could find work they saw as a calling it would improve their "life, health, and job satisfaction."[32]

While Calvin argued that callings were predestined, Wrzesniewski and her co-writers were offering a new path to fulfillment and all it required was finding a better job or even simpler, changing our mindset toward work. This idea spread and many people, including myself, started to search for our own modern callings.

In my first year at GE, in response to complaints from young employees, the company started building career pages on social media and investing in efforts to rebrand itself to potential employees. It wanted to present itself as a "cool" place for young people to build a career. One big reason companies like GE were willing to start making changes was the emerging tech industry in California. The tech industry was offering benefits that seemed too good to be true and this shift was led by Google, which gained attention by debuting on the 2007 Best Places to Work list at #1.

I remember reading the description and being envious of the benefits they offered:

> At Google you can do your laundry; drop off your dry cleaning; get an oil change, then have your car washed; work out in the gym; attend subsidized exercise classes; get a massage; study Mandarin, Japanese, Spanish, and French; and ask a personal concierge to arrange dinner reservations. Naturally you can get haircuts onsite. Want to buy a hybrid car? The company will give you $5,000 toward that environmentally friendly end.[33]

Google had made my list of prestigious companies, but it stood out from the rest. It was the only one at the time that promised that work could be fun. When I started at GE, my only understanding of a good relationship with work was "work-life balance," a concept popular in the early 2000s. While the term is still used today, it feels like it belongs to another era.

In the 2010s the expectation that work should be meaningful became a default expectation of college graduates. Young people no longer wanted simply to bide their time at a job but wanted a job with passion, purpose, and fun. By 2019, a survey of workers in the United States and Canada found that more than offering good pay and benefits, 78% of people thought "employers have a responsibility to keep employees mentally and physically well."[34]

Companies do their best to keep up with these growing expectations, which can be easily observed by scanning the career pages of well-known companies. This is what I did in early 2021, compiled a list of recruiting slogans from over 100 companies.[35] Some examples:

- Facebook: "Do the most meaningful work of your life"
- McKinsey: "Have a career that fits your calling"
- Ropes & Gray: "Write your own career story"
- Phillip Morris: "Change the world"
- Comcast: "Create the future with us"
- Microsoft: "Do what you love"
- Sears: "Jobs that transform your career"
- Citibank: "Discover your next adventure"

When I graduated in 2007, Google's promise to make work fun was the exception. Now every company is trying to be like Google. It's high stakes when an entire generation of workers not only thinks that work should be the most important thing in their lives, but also that it should enable them to thrive in all aspects of their life.

A study from the University of Sussex by professors Bailey and Madden should cast doubts on whether these expectations can be met. In their research, they did in-depth interviews with 135 individuals in 10 different professions about the most meaningful moments in their jobs. Their conclusion: "helping people find meaning in their work is complex and profound, going far beyond the relative superficialities of satisfaction or engagement." Their research found that instead of joy, meaningful experiences were "associated with mixed, uncomfortable, or even painful thoughts and feelings, not just a sense of unalloyed joy and happiness."[36]

Despite thinking I wanted fun and joy at work for most of my career, when I reflect on the most meaningful moments of my career, they involve overcoming obstacles, or getting through setbacks to complete something I didn't think I could.

This is much different than what most companies are promising and increasingly, what many people have come to expect out of work.

Wage-based Society

Sociologist André Gorz spent the latter half of the 20th century writing about the role of work in society. He argued that many countries had evolved into places where the primary way one gained "membership" in society was through formal work. He called these places "wage-based societies" where the central ethic was, "never mind what work you do, what counts is having a job."[37]

A powerful example of this kind of ethic can be seen when people refer to a parent who decides to become a full-time caretaker of their children as someone that "decides to stay home." This way of thinking leads to an oversimplification of how societies operate, assumptions on how people should live their lives, and ignorance of the realities and downsides of the "regular" way of working. Many people are surprised to find out that in the United States, one of the strongest "wage-based societies" in the world, only about 40% of adult Americans, or 106 million people, have jobs where they work more than 35 hours per week.[38]

Seeing the job as a central element of a good life and employment rates as a metric of a successful society was not a common assumption until after World War II. In 1946, the United States formalized this by passing the Full Employment Act "to promote maximum employment."[39]

This created a clear metric that everyone could use to judge a government's performance and today, political leaders do whatever possible to protect or create jobs. One striking example is from 2009 when U.S. President Barack Obama explicitly mentioned jobs as the reason why he did not want to pursue a more ambitious healthcare policy:

> *Everybody who supports single-payer healthcare says, 'Look at all this money we would be saving from insurance and paperwork.' That represents 1 million, 2 million, 3 million jobs of people who are working at Blue Cross Blue Shield or Kaiser or other places. What are we doing with them? Where are we employing them?*[40]

Regardless of whether single-payer healthcare would have improved lives or not, this decision shows that, at least in the United States, government leaders prefer to create or save jobs rather than doing anything that risks losing them. For Obama, it was also a smart decision, as the healthcare sector was one of the few areas that saw continued job growth after the 2008 recession, and the good "jobs numbers" were a key reason Obama was able to win re-election.

For most people, having a job is better than not having a job, and the costs of unemployment are well documented in academic studies. Researchers at the University of Stirling found that people who are unemployed can become less friendly, less hard-working, and less open to new experiences.[41] Another study showed that although unemployed men have much more free time, they volunteer less often than similarly employed men.[42]

Based on this analysis, you could conclude that jobs are good, full stop. Unfortunately, this way of thinking is challenged by the dramatic shifts in the ways people are working. In 2016, economists Lawrence Katz and Alan Kreuger highlighted a group of 30 million people categorized by the U.S. government as "alternative" or "nontraditional" workers and showed that they were responsible for nearly all of U.S. job growth from 2005 to 2015, adding nearly 10 million jobs.[43]

McKinsey & Company found similar trends across Europe and estimated that more than 100 million people across the United States and Europe are now "nontraditional" employees. McKinsey compared these workers to "traditional" employees and found that they were as satisfied or more satisfied across fifteen different work characteristics, such as income, independence, hours, flexibility, creativity, and even recognition.[44] Though this group is quite large, it doesn't have a cohesive voice, and people are often surprised to find that most of these "alternative" workers are quite happy.

In addition to ignoring this new way of working, we also ignore the enormous amount of wasted energy and effort that is a part of many jobs. In his book *Bullshit Jobs,* David Graeber detailed stories of people working in jobs where they were personally convinced that nothing they did was of value. However, if you find yourself in such a job, it is rarely worthwhile to point this out to other people.

My first experience with this was as an intern at a large corporation after my first year of college. A few weeks in, the Vice President told me he had a special project for me. He wanted me to spend the next couple of weeks going through boxes of documents. Rumor had it that one of the boxes contained a record of the repair work the company performed on one of Amelia Earhart's planes. At first, it felt cool to be working on this project for one of the leaders of the organization, but the excitement quickly faded as my fingers dried out several days into my search through the boxes.

When I tried to talk about the incredible amount of time I was wasting on this project, people quickly redirected my inquiry, saying, "It may suck, but you're getting something to put on your resume!" or "Everyone has to work, what are you supposed to do?" or "You should be grateful for being paid." No one wanted to grapple with this fundamental question: "Why the hell are so many grown adults spending their time on obviously pointless tasks?"

During my second internship at the same company in a different department, I shared a cubicle with a man in his 50s who spent five to six hours a day surfing the web and printing out articles about celebrities. One of the other interns brought a pillow and took daily naps in an abandoned cubicle in another area of the building. I had studied advanced math and physics thinking I would apply those skills, but instead I spent my summers doing simple math on Excel spreadsheets. The notion of spending the rest of my life doing mindless busywork horrified me and motivated me to keep searching for better options. It's also what drove me to try to break into strategy consulting where I wouldn't have to spend so much time proving I was willing to do things I didn't believe in.

Yet at McKinsey, proving your commitment to work came in a different flavor. The work was much more interesting, but it seemed that people were in an endless search to do more. In my first week on the job, my manager told me that I was expected to work 40–50 hours a week and I took her at her word. Yet most of my colleagues worked 50 to 60 hours a week or more.

My colleagues always laughed when I left the office at 5:30. "Paul can get away with it, he's just different," they would say. I thought I was simply more efficient and worried a little less. The reality was that I never bought into the wage-based mentality and could never fully commit to placing work at the center of my life.

Eventually, something would have to break.

4

Awakening

The ultimate way you and I get lucky is if you have some success early in life, you get to find out early it doesn't mean anything. – David Foster Wallace

I had no master plan to quit my job. Even now, several years after doing so, when people ask about my journey, I'm more confused than you might expect. Choosing to leave full-time work was not a single bold decision but a slow and steady awakening that the path I was on was not my path.

It's tempting to tell a simpler story. People want to hear about bold acts of courage, not years of feeling lost. On my way toward leaving my job, I never had a clear picture of my next step. Experiencing this makes it easy to spot these kinds of phases in other people's stories and I've done my best to highlight them in my writing and podcast.

My conclusion from this is simple: beyond the headlines of dramatic life changes are almost always longer, slower, and more interesting journeys.

Pebble in My Shoe

As I recovered from my health challenges, I entered a phase of restlessness typical of anyone that eventually makes a life change.

A friend, Khe Hy, provides a perfect description of this phase. Fifteen years into a successful career in finance, he walked away to find a new path. However, it took him a long time to make that decision. He reflected, "It definitely wasn't a sudden realization. It's a little bit like having a pebble in your shoe, where you're walking and something is off, and it's mildly uncomfortable."[45]

When he got raises or promotions the discomfort would subside but never disappear. Slowly, he became more curious about that feeling and realized that despite his external success, he had become a "passive participant" in his life. Eventually, this convinced him to embark on his own pathless path.

When I returned to work after regaining my health, I had discomfort that could only be described the way Khe put it, as a pebble in my shoe. It wasn't enough of a feeling to make me do anything dramatic, but it threw me off just enough that I was forced to pay attention to my life in a different way.

As I started to pay attention, I slowly came to realize the reality that I had been living in was an invisible bubble, one of my own creation. I started to push the edges of that reality and wasn't sure what would happen.

A Daily Reminder

If there are clear boundaries to behavior within a given field of endeavor, then there is also great freedom to adapt and imagine within those lines. These boundaries, however, should always be tested to see if they are actually still real. It takes conscious acts by individuals to test these edges. – David Whyte

After returning to work, I felt like I had gone through a major transformation, but to my colleagues, I appeared back to normal. I was physically present but detached. Rather than participating in meetings as a good team member, I observed them as a visiting anthropologist. I saw my colleagues with new eyes. *Are they happy? What kind of pain or challenges are they dealing with? Is this how they want to be spending their time?*

Once you ask these questions there is no going back. Not because of the contradictions in other people's lives, but because it makes it difficult to live in contradiction in your own life.

This inspired me to act. I wanted to design a career that worked for me and decided to start with a simple commitment, one inspired by a talk from Earl Jones, an MIT alumnus who had shared his leadership principles with my class in grad school. I remembered how he had a list of words that reminded him of what he values, something that popped up on his calendar every morning.

I followed his example and created a daily calendar entry of priorities for my life. First on my list was health. After recovering from my health challenges, I would do anything to stay healthy. Next, my head told me to list "career," but my heart told me to list it last. This simple decision was my first conscious commitment to exploring the possibility of a life not centered around work. My final list included four items: health, relationships, fun & creativity, and career. Since 2013, this list pops up on my phone at 8:30 a.m. each morning.

Staring at those four items, in that order, was scary. Without knowing it, I had embraced a question that would shape my decisions: "How do you design a life that doesn't put work first?"

The answer, my dear reader, is simple. You start underachieving at work.

You stop setting an alarm and you cancel morning meetings because the energy gained is worth fighting for. You start working remotely on Fridays without asking because the extra 24 hours with your grandmother is worth it. You start taking naps at the office because there's a nap room and someone has to use it, right?

I felt like a rebel, like I was doing something wrong. At the same time, I had the sense that taking ownership of my life in this way, especially to prioritize my health, was something worth doing.

Instead of being consumed with thoughts about work and my next step, I had time to continue to experiment, and in the space that emerged, a creative energy entered which started to become a central force in my life.

A Fool's Journey

Creativity requires faith. Faith requires that we relinquish control.
– Julia Cameron

As I started to test my boundaries, I split into two different versions of myself. One, "Default Path Paul," focused on continuing my career, looking for the next job. The other, "Pathless Path Paul," was finding his footing and starting to pay attention to the clues that were showing up. Clues that would lead me not to another job, but to another life.

The first time I acted on one of these clues was during a conversation with a career coach in Boston. She shared how much she loved what she did. Her infectious energy made me want to know more.

One benefit of having learned to be a world-class hoop-jumper is being able to support friends. Most people hate thinking about career decisions, and I have always volunteered to help anyone that asked. I told the coach how much I enjoyed this and said that maybe one day I could do what she was doing. She looked at me quizzically and said, "it sounds like you're already a coach, though?"

Her comment rocked me. She urged me to try coaching as a side gig. I spent the next few minutes making excuses for why this was not possible but I think I had been waiting for someone like her to push me in a new direction. I finally had somewhere to direct my emergent creative energy and I told her that I accepted the challenge.

It would be a while until I "launched" the career coaching experiment, but I got to work immediately. I started by building a website, Careerswithpaul.com, and writing several articles about why I enjoyed helping people with careers. I tinkered with this project for several months and lost myself in the flow of work at my desk, sneaking in a few hours whenever I could. I'd go home and keep working on it. This phase of writing and creating was thrilling. It was a sharp contrast with my day job where I was working hard, but only in safe, predictable ways.

Instead of announcing this work to the world, however, Default Path Paul had orchestrated another job change, a position in New York City helping to build a consulting practice that provided services to CEOs and board members of large companies. Despite the obvious shift in my interests and energy, I was still searching for that elusive dream job and had not yet considered becoming self-employed.

There was no dream job to be found but as soon as I moved to New York, the energy of the city supercharged every other aspect of my life. I started exercising, wearing better clothes, and feeling more confident. On the coaching front, I joined a two-year mentorship program for first-generation college students and finally sent an email announcing the career coaching side gig to 100 of my closest friends and family. Sending that email was terrifying because it was like a coming-out party for Pathless Path Paul, a side of me that I had previously kept hidden.

I landed my first two paid coaching clients, and I loved the challenge of doing something new and on my own. It led me to do many more experiments. Over the next year, I launched a group coaching workshop, created an online course on resumes, started sharing my writing publicly, helped several clients navigate career and life shifts, and was even invited to give two paid talks on careers.

My view of the world was shifting and it was both exciting and disorienting. Austin Kleon, a prolific creator and writer, says that "creative work runs on uncertainty; it runs on not knowing what you're doing."[46] The creative work of finding a new life path is similar. I acknowledged as much in that email announcing my coaching work: "So here I am. I'm going to pursue this on the side and I wanted to share it with you first. Do I know where this will take me? No, but I'm excited to find out."

I took more responsibility for my life and started questioning my beliefs about work. When we talk about our jobs we often say, "I'm learning a lot!" In the first few years working in consulting, this was true. I grew in so many areas: writing, giving better presentations, communication skills, and research. A few years into the path, however, the things I was incentivized to learn became specific to the organization, such as navigating political conflicts and adopting behaviors, dress, and attitudes that signaled I might be a future company leader. I sucked at these things and my motivation tanked.

Daniel Vassallo describes experiencing a similar shift ten years into his career at Amazon: "Everything was going well and getting better. But despite all this, my motivation to go to work each morning was decreasing – almost in an inverse trend to my career and income growth." He came to the conclusion that "only intrinsic motivation lasts" and decided to leave a comfortable six-figure salary behind and create a life designed around flexible work, his interests, and his family.[47]

My lack of motivation at work made it easy to stay focused on my side projects despite not knowing where they were headed. The only way through this kind of uncertainty is to embrace what author and educator George Leonard called "the spirit of the fool." He argued that when you start learning anything new it will make you "feel clumsy, that you'll take literal or figurative pratfalls. There's no way around it."[48]

I liked feeling like a fool and the excitement that comes with learning something new. The only problem? I was miserable at my job.

Pushing Forward

It took a year and a half for me to admit I did not enjoy my job. I had spent years crafting an idea of who I thought I should be and working hard to find jobs that matched this idea. It was hard to admit that the foundation that I thought I had been building was incredibly fragile.

The first time I voiced an intention to "go work on my own" was in an annual performance evaluation with my manager. In a high-rise office overlooking the skyscrapers in New York, I acknowledged that I might be in the wrong place. He said something about me struggling to embrace the culture, and instead of arguing with him, I confessed, "My heart isn't in it."

I told him about my experiments with coaching and how the excitement I felt outside of work contrasted with the growing cynicism and frustration I experienced at work. For the first time, I was honest with my manager and with myself. As I shared my reflections, I blamed myself, and unexpectedly, I lost the ability to speak, finding myself on the verge of tears. While I didn't know it then, this was the first step toward letting go of my deep attachment to the default path.

I returned to my office and sat at my desk, staring blankly at my screen.

If you had told me when I was building that spreadsheet of dream jobs during college that not only would I work for several of those companies, but also directly with some of the most famous CEOs in the world, I would have been shocked. But I also would have thought that was exactly what I wanted.

As I sat there, I didn't know how to want it anymore.

I had been hired to help build a consulting division. The success I achieved in my first year earned me a raise and I was asked to develop a proposal for a new career path for our growing group. At the time, I felt like I had a future at the company. In my second year, I started working on an internal project meant to take three months. As it dragged on for more than a year, however, things started to fall apart. I became frustrated with the snail's pace and that's when the pebble in my shoe feeling became too powerful to ignore.

From my perspective now, I had no future at the company, and by the time I had that conversation about my performance with my manager, things were already headed south. Yet I was still working hard on my proposal for promotion, outlining a multi-year career path for my position. Based on the experiences of others who leave the default path, this stage of contradiction is common. You take a last stand, doubling down on the existing path despite all evidence that it is no longer working.

My biggest barrier was my inability to imagine an alternative life. My creative experiments were exciting, but they didn't suggest an obvious next step. It was easier to aim toward another raise or promotion than daring to ask myself deeper questions.

A passage from William Reilly's book *How To Avoid Work*, published in 1949, captures my reality at the time:

Your life is too short and too valuable to fritter away in work.

If you don't get out now, you may end up like the frog that is placed in a pot of fresh water on the stove. As the temperature is gradually increased, the frog feels restless and uncomfortable, but not uncomfortable enough to jump out. Without being aware that a chance is taking place, he is gradually lulled into unconsciousness.

Much the same thing happens when you take a person and put him in a job which he does not like. He gets irritable in his groove. His duties soon become a monotonous routine that slowly dulls his senses. As I walk into offices, through factories and stores, I often find myself looking into the expressionless faces of people going through mechanical motions. They are people whose minds are stunned and slowly dying.[49]

My path was suffocating part of me that I wanted to let breathe.

I had to do something.

What Am I Worth?

Even though I had said I wanted to work "on my own," based on my actions, I wasn't there yet. In the months after I sat in my manager's office on the verge of tears, I did what I always did when I felt frustrated. I started looking for another job. I still thought the perfect job was just around the corner.

Another consulting firm in New York seemed to offer a way forward. I read a book by the firm's founder outlining a new way of running a company centered around self-organization. The ideas excited me. After a number of great interviews with the firm, I reached the phase of an interview when you are about to receive an offer. Typically, I would be telling myself a story about how it was the perfect next step in my career. This time things felt different. The leader of the team called me to discuss the details. He was direct, "We want you to join our team, but we can only offer you $50,000 less than you make now."

This was a blow to the ego. I was worth more. Definitely $50,000 more.

He argued that since I was passionate about the work, it was worth taking a pay cut. I pretended that this was reasonable and told him I needed a few days to think about it. I hung up the phone and sat there. I was rattled. What the hell was I doing? Was I really trying to find work I cared about or was I just trying to move forward like I always did?

The low salary offer was a blessing in disguise. It forced me to think about money. Making more money was not one of the priorities on the list I read on my phone every morning, so why was I so attached to what I thought I was worth?

In 2008, attorney Kenneth Feinberg was appointed to a position in which he set the salaries of bank executives involved in the global financial crisis. He had to inform executives who made $5 million the previous year that they would only be making $1 million in the upcoming year. He expected them to be frustrated but understand, given the broader challenges in the economy. That's not what happened. Most were outraged. He realized that "these corporate officials viewed their compensation as the sole barometer of self-worth." He wasn't lowering their salaries; he was dealing a blow to the essence of who they thought they were.[50]

I claimed not to care about money, but the truth was that I was more like those executives than I thought.

I turned down the offer and started to ask harder questions. Why was I trying to get a raise when I knew I was not in a good environment? What was I seeking? Why did I keep changing jobs every two years? What was that pebble in my shoe really telling me?

These questions inspired an idea: *what if I paired making less with working less?*

I started to imagine a new path. Why not attempt to do the work I wanted to do as a freelancer while also having more flexibility and control over my life?

5

Breaking Free

Some people inherit values and practices as a house they inhabit; some of us have to burn down that house, find our own ground, build from scratch, even as a psychological metamorphosis. – Rebecca Solnit

Not Who I Wanted To Be

After rejecting the job offer, I took time to reflect on what I wanted. I revisited a letter I had written for a leadership class during business school. In it, I defined a leader broadly as someone that could be a "role model in all aspects of their life." I specifically listed nine principles, a collection of phrases, quotes, ideas, and beliefs that I hoped to embody throughout my career. Some examples included a desire to lead with empathy, to embrace humility, to inject humor wherever possible, to avoid becoming too serious, to prioritize learning, to think independently, and to create memorable experiences for others through my work.

I decided to turn this into a self-assessment and reviewed each of the nine principles, scoring myself on a scale of one to ten. A few areas earned low scores. First, my curiosity and passion for learning at work were nonexistent. Second, I was struggling to think independently in a positive way. I was becoming cynical and confrontational rather than looking for ways to have a positive impact. Finally, I had become too serious about work. At some point, I had lost my sense of humor and was spending far too much time getting caught up in company politics.

Simply put, I was a curmudgeon at work, increasingly cynical about the intentions of leaders, not learning anything beyond the latest office gossip.

Deep down I knew these things, but I hadn't chosen to face what I knew. Putting a score on a page showed me that I was struggling to become the kind of person I thought I could be. Jerry Colonna, an investor turned executive coach, asks his clients this question, "How are you complicit in creating the conditions you say you don't want?" After the reflection, I knew that I was complicit. I also knew that if I wanted things to change, it was solely up to me.

In business school, I created a vision of the kind of leader and person I wanted to be, and five years later I realized I was headed in the wrong direction. When I wrote that paper, my model of the world was one in which my principles would triumph over my environment. If those principles still mattered to me, which they did, I needed to get more creative about how I could bring them forth in my life and career.

Email from Sarasota

"I think it's time to move on."

I wrote that sentence in a hotel room in Sarasota, Florida. I had just arrived for the weekend to attend a friend's wedding. I opened my laptop to check work emails before heading down to the pool and saw several emails from my manager.

There was nothing special about those emails, but that day I couldn't pretend to care about the latest client crisis. Anyone who has worked in client or customer-facing jobs knows that the work mostly focuses on reacting to ongoing mini-crises. Almost everyone agrees that these issues are not all that important, but almost no one can stop themselves from reacting to each one with equal enthusiasm and panic.

I told my manager that I found his emails unnecessarily aggressive. He disagreed and we argued a bit back and forth. At the end of one exchange, I added, "I think I should move on."

He interpreted this remark as a formal resignation and had probably been expecting this moment since I had choked up in his office. I had no conscious intention to quit right then, but I couldn't muster up a single ounce of energy to tell him otherwise.

I sat in my hotel room and didn't know what to think. I could stop what I had set in motion, but I didn't. I felt excited but confused. Did I just quit? I walked down to the pool to start the wedding weekend, saw a friend, and said, "I think I just quit my job."

So much of life is like this. We are surprised at the moment something happens, but looking back, we realize that everything makes sense. Losing my grandfather, getting rejected from jobs repeatedly, never finding the right fit, facing health challenges and hard questions were all events that sent me in an inevitable direction that was only obvious upon reflection.

When I quit, it was the only thing left to do. It took me 10 seconds at the bottom of an email.

Commuting in the Blob

I stayed in the job for three months to train my replacement and help the team transition. It was about three months too long.

No single day stands out. I stuck to my daily routine, arriving each morning at the 7 train subway platform. I boarded the train for the single-stop journey from Queens to Manhattan. Then I slid my body into the masses of people and became part of a massive blob of workers making our way into the mecca of work.

Each day I searched for signs of life. I would force a smile and look around to see if anyone noticed. No one ever did. So I gave up and adopted the neutral uninterested smirk that everyone seemed to understand was the proper way to be.

When we pulled into Grand Central, the blob became active with people jockeying for position to embark on their unique paths through the labyrinth of stairs and tunnels. I had my own special route and knew the speed and angles to make it to my desk as fast as possible. On my first day at this job, the first time I had worked in New York City, I paused and took a deep breath as I walked through the center of the station. It felt special. It was special. Now I wanted no part of it, but each morning I continued to go through the motions. The building I worked in, now known as the MetLife building, was built next to Grand Central Station in 1963 and was universally panned at the time. Architecture critic Ada Louise Huxtable called it "a lesson in how to be mediocre without really trying."[51]

Twenty stories up in that building was my office, its furnishings dating back to the 1970s or 1980s. The offices of the senior partners, still mostly men, were located along the building's outside walls. Decades after the offices had been built, their positions and sizes were still clear markers of importance. My small office was a step up from the cubicles, but I was still years away from having a real office. I always appreciated the clarity of these distinctions. So many companies seem afraid to make these power dynamics visible, disguising them behind open offices and casual dress codes.

In those final months, I was in a liminal space between two worlds. I had decided to take a leap to a different path but had not yet changed direction. I struggled to process how I was feeling, held captive by accumulated frustration and anxiety. When I thought about my future, everything came up blank. I did my best to pretend I knew what I was doing, but for the first time in my life, I was operating without a script.

Was I doing the right thing?

It didn't really matter. There was no turning back. I was embarking on a new path, and I had no choice but to find out. As the final day at work approached, I pretended to be excited, but I was merely existing, one day at a time.

Too Smart for Burnout

I told myself I was smarter than other people. I knew what I was good at. I always took all of my vacation days. Didn't work crazy hours. Made time for friends and family. Changed jobs when I stopped learning. I had done all these things with the idea that this was how I would not only avoid burning out but that I would thrive. I wanted to hack the system and make it work for me. On my final day of work the feelings that flowed through my body told me I wasn't so clever.

The first day after leaving my job I started my day like any other, waking up and making coffee. Our apartment in Long Island City had a beautiful view of the Manhattan skyline. My roommate and I had decided to move there six months prior, hoping to upgrade our apartment for the same rent we had been paying in Manhattan. It was a beautiful space. Yet as I looked out at the skyscrapers where I had been working just a day earlier, it felt weird. I was suddenly an outside observer not yet able to make sense of what I had left behind.

I spent the next couple of hours wandering around the apartment, eventually sat down, and opened my computer. Something told me I needed to write and as soon as I started typing, an emotional flood of energy took over my body. Years of resentment, frustration, and confusion demanded to be released.

While working, I always sensed that these feelings were there, but the daily inertia of a life centered around work kept them hidden. Now, without a plan and without anywhere to show up, I had to feel the full force of my emotions.

I gained my composure and kept writing. The words seemed to flow from my heart and as I got about halfway down the first page a word came out that surprised me.

Burnout.

I couldn't be burnt out. I was too smart! Burnout is for investment bankers and lawyers working every weekend and logging 80-hour weeks. I tried to explain it away but I couldn't. This was the only word that seemed to capture the brokenness I had felt over the previous year.

The word burnout was coined in the 1970s by Herbert Freudenberger, an American psychologist who studied workers in free health clinics. He found that the prime candidates for burnout were those who were "dedicated and committed," trying to balance their need to give, to please others, and to work hard. He noticed that when there was added pressure from superiors, people often hit a breaking point.[52]

Throughout the 1980s, burnout was studied across most types of work and by the end of the decade, there were hundreds of definitions. Freudenberger seemed distraught by this fact but still wanted to understand what might cause burnout. He was intrigued by Professor Cary Cherniss' definition of burnout as "the bureaucratic infringement on a professional's autonomy" and thought that the right way to think about burnout was to focus on the disconnect between an individual and the culture of the company in which they worked.[53]

This also meant that burnout might be unavoidable which motivated Freudenberger to ask two provocative questions:

1. What if the value system of the institution is diametrically opposed to the values, ethics, and competencies of the individual

professional?

2. What if the individual professional seeks to live up to the external, organizationally imposed criteria of what constitutes success and achievement, but is unable to do so?

These questions still linger in our workplaces, and in the years since Freudenberger asked them, our economy has continued to shift towards the type of helping professions that are similar to the workers he studied in the health clinics.

People dedicate themselves to being "good workers," and being successful means keeping clients, customers, and managers happy while fitting into a company's cultural norms. Unfortunately, success for the company does not always align with what is best for the person, and over time, a disconnect can emerge. This is what happened to me.

At that last job, I wasn't a team player and I could have tried harder to say the right things, dress the right way, or spend more time pleasing my manager. But I couldn't do it. The norms of the organization were pulling me too far away from the person I wanted to be and the energy I used to manage this disconnect undermined anything good I had to offer.

A German report on burnout found that when burned out, people "may start being cynical about their working conditions and their colleagues..." and may "...distance themselves emotionally and start feeling numb about their work."[54] This is the tricky thing about burnout. If you are suffering from burnout, you are likely not thriving at work, and over time it's easy to see yourself as the cause. Add to this the common assumption that you should never leave a job too soon and you get a world in which millions of people are experiencing the slow, marginal creep of burnout and have no way out.

Luckily, I found my way out and as I finished writing the piece, I felt a sense of relief wash over my body. I was able to forgive myself for some of my failures in that job and with that, I was ready to move forward.

The Dynamics of Mourning

But under the hardness of that armor there is the tenderness of genuine sadness.
   – Pema Chodron

To celebrate leaving my job I decided to take an extended trip to Europe. As I was booking the flights, I initially typed in dates two weeks apart, but then realized I had no obligations to return to. Before this trip, I had never traveled anywhere for more than two weeks. As I extended the dates to five weeks on the booking app, sirens sounded in my head. This was the first of many experiences in which I pushed past the default setting of how I was supposed to be living.

In the first week, I watched an incredible sunset in Florence, sharing a cheap bottle of wine with a friend I had met from Ecuador earlier that day. As the colors exploded over the city, I was filled with joy and excitement about the new adventure in front of me.

The next day, however, I woke up with one of the worst colds I've ever had. It was as if my body was saying, "not so fast!" Professor Freudenberger noted in his research that for some people, burnout involves the "dynamics of mourning" due to dealing with the "loss of something within yourself, something you treasured and valued, your ideals."[55] Freudenberger argued that recovering from burnout involves a grieving process to let go of those ideals. I had not factored this into my journey and did not expect how hard it would hit me in that first month. I settled into a slower pace as my trip through Europe shifted from a celebration to rest and recovery.

On the final weekend of my trip, I spent the July 4th holiday in the small village of Praiano on the Amalfi Coast in Italy. A few people I had met at a dinner the night before joined me at the beach. One woman was a successful designer working at IDEO in Chicago and we started talking about why I had left my job. I told her I was excited about having space to experiment, explore ideas, and not have to work for someone else. She was confused and asked, "why not just find another job?"

A year earlier I would have shared my career ambitions and added her on LinkedIn. But instead, I answered, "Good question, I'm not sure." I was living in the present, taking it one day at a time. It felt good. I was also nervous.

I was heading back to the United States, and I would have to see if I could turn those intentions into reality.

Fool with a Sign

Reality was waiting in New York. I had quit my job and didn't have any work lined up. After ten years of being on the default path, I felt exposed.

Living in New York City didn't help. Being in one of the most expensive cities in the world, the pressure to make money was intense. When I was getting paid on a steady basis, the relationship between making money and my motivation was hard to understand. Without a paycheck, the combination of insecurity, fear, and my desire to prove myself made it much clearer. This ignited a period of frenzied activity, one which I've noticed is a common stage for people that leave their jobs without an income.

I started proactively pursuing freelance projects and said yes to every opportunity. The first gig was one that paid me $1,000 to walk around New York City, find people wearing Allbird brand shoes, and ask them four questions. On my first day, I struggled to find people by randomly walking around the city. On day two, I took a different approach, buying a large cardboard sign and writing in big letters, "Do you own Allbirds?" I held up the sign at the farmer's market in Union Square Park and started finding people. Despite some embarrassment, I was able to laugh at myself and have fun with it. Being a fool with a sign landed me my first paycheck and it also helped serve as a ritualistic shift away from a life of dress shirts and formalities to one that was a little more free.

I landed a more substantial project a few months later working with a former professor launching a non-profit in Boston. As I signed the contract, I made the first substantial dent in the fear that I would fail. What a relief! I even ended up landing a few smaller projects and in one of the months, I made more in a single month than I did in any month I had as an employee. The project in Boston also convinced me to move from New York back to Boston, helping to cut down on my cost of living. These things all gave me a lot of confidence that my experiment to work on my own was something that had potential, and I started to ease into my journey.

As my money anxieties receded, I realized I wanted to go deeper.

Not with freelance work, but in my life. In those first six months, I experienced a remarkable sense of freedom and ownership over my life. Most days I decided when, where, and how I worked. It differed radically from how I had spent my days on my previous path and this made me curious enough to consider a question that would push me deeper into an exploration of my relationship to work.

Am I a Worker?

During the first few months of self-employment, I read an article that jolted my reality. Titled, "If work dominated your every moment, would life be worth living?" the philosopher Andrew Taggart offered a powerful question that spoke to the underlying tension I lived with for most of my adult life.

By my late 20s, I had oriented my entire life around work. I was always thinking about how I could get a better job or a higher salary. I had launched a side gig helping people navigate their careers and started writing about how the working world could be better. I could only afford my expensive New York City apartment because I was earning a high income, and my social life was spent with similarly high-earning friends.

At the time I could not imagine any other existence. Where I lived, what I did, how I thought about money, and the people I hung out with were all connected with my work identity. But if someone had asked me if work took over "every moment" of my life, I would have declared "not me!"

Yet when I became self-employed, I was surprised at how strongly I had internalized a worker identity. As I struggled to find my first project, I felt guilty when I wasn't working during typical work hours Monday through Friday. When I started working remotely on my first project, I had 100% control over when and how I did the work, but quickly fell into a routine of going to a coworking office five days a week. Many self-employed people are surprised to find that once they no longer have to work for anyone else, they still have a manager in their head.

As I started to experiment with how I spent my time, Taggart's question remained in my head. I was fascinated by his claim that we lived in a time of "total work," a state of existence in which work is such a powerful force that almost everyone ends up identifying as a worker first and foremost. The idea of total work was inspired by the German philosopher Josef Pieper, who first wrote about it in his book *Leisure, The Basis of Culture*. Writing in Germany after World War II, Pieper was shocked at how people were eager to throw themselves into work without pausing to reflect on what kind of world they wanted to build. To Pieper, this was evidence that German society had abandoned a connection to a traditional form of leisure.[56]

Pieper argued that for most of history, leisure was one of the most important parts of life for people in many cultures. He noted that the ancient Greek translation for "work" was literally "not-at-leisure." In Aristotle's own words, "we are not-at-leisure in order to be-at-leisure." Now, this is flipped. We work to earn time off and see leisure as a break from work. Pieper pointed out that people "mistake leisure for idleness, and work for creativity." To Pieper, leisure was above work. It was "a condition of the soul," and the "disposition of receptive understanding, of contemplative beholding, and immersion – in the real."[57]

As I embraced the freedom of self-employment, I was opening up to this kind of leisure but was also still dealing with the lasting power of a world of total work that I had fully embraced, one where my perceived value was derived from my ability to keep working. Yet Taggart's question remained a daily companion:

> *"If work dominated your every moment, would life be worth living?"*

My answer was becoming a clear "no," but I didn't know what this meant for my life. Eventually, I reached out to Taggart directly and he proposed three more specific questions:

1. Are you a worker?
2. If you are not a worker, then who are you?
3. Given who you are, what life is sufficient?

While these questions were terrifying, I was ready to start asking them seriously. According to Taggart, living in a world dominated by total work undermines the "playful contemplation concerned with our asking, pondering and answering the most basic questions of existence."[58] As I gained confidence on my new path, I was starting to be able to ask these questions and was open to the possibilities that were about to emerge.

Possibility

After six months of freelancing, I had a nice ending point for several projects and decided to design my own non-work sabbatical. I abandoned the responsibility of being a "worker" and instead woke up each morning and did what I felt like doing. Most days I woke up without an alarm clock, worked out when I felt like it and wandered around the city on what used to be "normal" workdays. For the first time, I was able to deeply know the type of leisure that Pieper wrote about.

This was also confusing. When people asked how my work was going, I offered a hand-wavey response, trying to hide my guilt of pursuing such a radical experiment.

Yet my excitement for life grew and my curiosity soared. I felt drawn to creative projects again as I had been in New York. One was a blog. For months I had intended to bring together the writing I had been doing under the name of "Boundless," but had been distracted by freelance work. With time and a nudge from my friend Greg, I finally launched the site as well as a podcast of the same name. I didn't intend to make money with these projects which still felt like the "wrong" approach, but I was finding work I really enjoyed doing. I was having fun.

For the first time, I was living the intentions I had set years earlier that popped up every day on my phone: health, relationships, fun & creativity, and career. In my official, public story I was doing freelance consulting, but really I was taking my first sabbatical, learning how it felt to live life not oriented around work.

My projects started to transcend my understanding of work. In my life as a full-time employee, work was a Monday through Friday thing I tried to minimize. Now it didn't matter when I worked on my projects. They were energizing and rarely left me drained. For a long time, I had thought that if I wanted to be happier with my work, I just needed a better job. Now I saw that I just wanted a different relationship with work, one that, at least for now, didn't come with a paycheck.

A lot of our confusion around work results from ideas like meaningful work and the widespread belief that we can always make money doing something we love. The blogger Marc Winn supercharged this idea in a viral meme. Winn translated a diagram created in 2011 by Andrés Zuzunaga and replaced the Spanish word for "purpose" with "Ikigai."[59] In Winn's version, finding your Ikigai means aligning what you love, what you are good at, what the world needs, and what can be paid for.[60] You can see these two diagrams here:

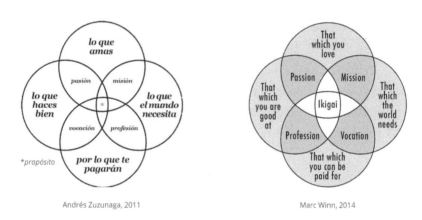

Andrés Zuzunaga, 2011   Marc Winn, 2014

While many people have embraced this version of Ikigai, having discovered work I love doing that doesn't come with a paycheck, I've realized that it's wishful thinking. Plus, in Japanese, Ikigai is none of these things. Rather, its best translation is simply that it is a "reason for being" or "something to live for."[61] Similar to expectations around meaningful work, far too many people limit their imagination of work worth doing to things that either come with a paycheck, require qualifications, or have a socially accepted story of impact.

If I limited myself in the same way I would have lost all energy to continue. For me, I was finding that the act of creation was the reward itself. The philosopher Erich Fromm has argued that "creative union," or when "man unites himself with the world in the process of creation," is a way to experience love.[62] I would have thought this completely absurd if I had not felt the depths of my connection to the world in those months.

After a few months of this, I was completely open to the world yet also starting to worry about eventually needing to make money again. Despite this, I had booked another month-long trip, this time to Asia. About a week before the trip, an opportunity emerged, one that would expand my own imagination about what was possible on my path.

A freelance recruiting company called me a week before the trip about an urgent client request to help them build a consulting skills training program. At first, I was disappointed because it was a project I wanted to do. I told the person I was leaving and that he needed to find someone else. He urged me to apply regardless. I decided to come up with terms that I would say "hell yes!" if they agreed. I would work on the job for 10–15 hours a week, for double the rate I had been charging other clients, and I would do it from Asia. I expected them to quickly reject this but to my surprise, they said yes within an hour of sending my proposal.

Over the next few weeks, I worked in small bursts from a tiny Airbnb in government housing in Singapore, a luxury hotel in Kuala Lumpur, a café on a cliff in Bali, and the beach on an island in Thailand. In Bali, I commuted 30 seconds down the cliff from the $20 surfer hostel I had rented to the café. I opened my laptop and drank thick, Balinese coffee while watching surfers in the distance. This weird kind of life was only possible due to the internet, and I could not have imagined it even one month earlier.

In stepping away from my temporary identity as a freelance consultant, I let myself fully lean into what I would later call the pathless path. As I wandered Asia, my mind exploded with possibility. If it was possible to work from a laptop in Bali, what else had I not yet considered?

My imagination was open, and I was ready to see where it might take me.

6

The First Steps

The one who wonders not only does not know, he is intimately sure that he does not know, and he understands himself as being in a position of not-knowing. But this un-knowing is not the kind that brings resignation. The one who wonders is one who sets out on a journey, and this journey goes along with the wonder: not only that he stops short for a moment, and is silent, but also that he persists in searching. – Joseph Pieper

Prototype Your Leap

Our tendency to glorify and simplify stories of people quitting their jobs convinces far too many people that this move is only possible for uniquely courageous people.

My story is not one of courage, but of pragmatic and safe experiments, experiences, and questioning over several years. This approach, one of prototyping a change, is not only a better way to think about taking bold leaps but is quite common across many people's stories.

79

I've developed a keen eye for seeing when there's more to a story beneath its surface. For example, when I saw an article by author and designer John Zeratsky titled, "I Quit My Job to Sail Around Central America for 18 Months," I knew immediately there was more. So I interviewed him for the podcast to find out just how he got to that point.

His story started several years earlier. He said, "before we left…we would take small sailing trips, we would go somewhere for one night… Later that year we would do that for a long weekend, then for a week, and then for two weeks. A couple of years before we left on the 'big trip' we went for two months."[63] It took several years and many smaller trips to decide that sailing for more than a year was something they definitely wanted to do.

This kind of approach, focused not on being brave, but instead on eliminating risk, is common for people who take unconventional paths. I hadn't set out to prototype a life beyond full-time work, but through freelance projects, coaching, paid speaking, writing, and connecting with people online, I achieved the same result. I knew what it felt like to work "differently" and make money on my own, and I learned to appreciate the "spirit of the fool" on an uncertain path. This was powerful because it helped me expand my perception of what I thought possible.

Diania Merriam had a similar experience in the years before she decided to leave her sales job. Her imagination was first sparked when she discovered the financially independent, retire early (FIRE) community. FIRE changed how she thought about money, which helped her get out of $30,000 of debt in 11 months. After that, she negotiated with her manager to work remotely, which enabled her to move to Ohio and buy a house.

Without debt, she felt less dependent on her job and after a successful year in her sales job, she requested a two-month unpaid sabbatical instead of a pay raise.[64] Her dream was to walk the Camino de Santiago, a famous pilgrimage in Spain. She was prepared to quit if her manager said "no," but to her surprise, she said "yes" without much hesitation.

The trip was a powerful experience and her imagination continued to expand as she experienced more ownership over her life. These experiences inspired her to launch a conference called EconoMe for people like her who were reimagining the American Dream, and she continued to engage in many other projects beyond her job. A couple of years after launching the conference she was asked to help host a daily finance podcast. She was eventually offered a paid position to be the lead host. Although the pay was only one-third of her salary at the time, she thought it was a "manageable risk" and decided to use it as an opportunity to finally quit her job and explore the full potential of self-employment.

Over several years, Diania was inadvertently prototyping new ways of living life. When she decided to quit, she already had some things she knew she wanted to work on such as her conference and an understanding of what it might feel like to live and work in a different way.

Doing even a small experiment is scary, but the payoff can be profound. When I hosted a group coaching session in New York, I was extremely nervous. I had never done anything like it before, but by the end of the night, I knew that bringing together curious people around questions I was excited to explore was something worth being uncomfortable for. The more experiments I've done, the more comfortable I have become, and this gives me more freedom to try new things without being afraid.

For most people, life is not based on all-or-nothing leaps of faith. That's a lie we tell ourselves so that we can remain comfortable in our current state. We simplify life transitions down to single moments because the real stories are more complex, harder to tell and attract less attention. The headline, "Quits To Live on a Sailboat" seems more impressive and is easier to talk about than "Couple Slowly and Purposefully Tests Out a Life Transition while Aggressively Saving Money over Five Years." As a result, we hear fewer of the real stories, most of which include some kind of prototyping.

By experimenting with different ways of showing up in the world and making small, deliberate changes, we can open ourselves up to the unexpected opportunities, possibilities, and connections that might tell us what comes next.

Wonder Tips the Scales

Many people dislike some parts of their jobs. But they stay in their jobs because their suffering is familiar. To change would be to trade the known for the unknown and change brings discomfort in hard to predict forms. So people avoid change and develop coping strategies. They learn to sidestep the manipulative manager, or like me, change jobs every couple of years, plan vacations, stay busy, and get drunk during the weekend. Play this game long enough without becoming too burned out and you might end up getting promoted.

We can explain this strategy with a simple equation:

```
Uncertain Discomfort < Certain Discomfort + Coping Mechanism
```

In other words, given sufficient coping strategies, people will be willing to tolerate consistent levels of misery for long stretches of time. Is there anything that can override this? In my conversations with people who have made changes in their life, one thing seems to work reliably: wonder.

Wonder is the state of being open to the world, its beauty, and potential possibilities. With wonder, the need to cope becomes less important and the discomfort on the current path becomes more noticeable. The equation becomes:

```
Uncertain Discomfort + Wonder > Certain Discomfort
```

In thoughts about the future, worry is traded for wonder. People stop thinking about worst-case scenarios and begin to imagine the benefits of following an uncertain path. They get curious about who they might become if they embrace discomfort and are filled with a sense of urgency that says, "if I don't do this now, I might regret it."

Michael Ashcroft had worked as a consultant in the energy sector for almost ten years when he decided to quit and become self-employed. An experience with burnout motivated him to prototype different kinds of work that might enable him to leave his job like teaching online courses and coaching. Before he left his job, he told me, "I have a suspicion that a whole bunch of energy will get unlocked. I'll just start doing things, and creating things and talking to people, and going to places...that I cannot fundamentally imagine right now, and it will be that stuff that shapes my life going forward...I am curious what else will show up."[65] He was able to take the leap because he had tapped into the power of wonder, enabling him to be excited about an uncertain future.

The travel writer Rolf Potts first experienced the power of possibility and wonder at the end of an eight-month trip he took around the United States when he was young. It was the first time he "[let] the journey breathe" and embraced a slower pace of travel. He described a complete transformation: "Who I was before and after was best defined as I was uncertain before the trip and I was confident after the trip in terms of what the potential for life was."[66]

I experienced a similar feeling after working remotely and traveling through Asia for that month. My path was more uncertain than ever, but the possibilities exploding in my mind overwhelmed any chance for my insecurity to take over.

One challenge to embracing possibility is knowing when to override what psychology professors Gilovich and Davidai call our "'ought to' self." This is the voice that helps us follow through on commitments but can also keep us from making changes in our lives. This is the voice that might convince you that leaving a job is an abdication of responsibility. We "ought to" keep working. This impulse is helpful most of the time, but compounded over one's life it stops us from moving towards what Gilovich and Davidai call our "ideal self." When people reflect on their lives, these are the things that people regret most – not moving towards their ideal selves. The professors argue that people rarely regret the things they do in their lives. This is exactly because of the power of our "ought to" selves – even if we fail, we tend to take immediate action to fix those mistakes.[67]

The author Gretchen Rubin decided to override her "ought to" self when she said, "I've come to a point where I'd rather fail as a writer than succeed as a lawyer, and I need to try and fail or try and succeed, but I need to do it."[68] Rubin attended Yale Law School, clerked for Sandra Day O'Connor on the Supreme Court, and was at the start of a high-paying and promising law career. Yet, she understood that if she kept going and never took a chance on becoming a writer, she would regret it.

Making life changes requires overcoming the discomfort of not knowing what will happen. Facing uncertainty, we make long mental lists of things that might go wrong and use these as the reasons why we must stay on our current path. Learning to have a healthy distrust of this impulse and knowing that even if things go wrong, we might discover things worth finding can help us open ourselves up to the potential for wonderful things to happen. Only when you reach this state are you at the same point as Rubin was, with no questions left about taking the next step. And don't worry, even if you do screw up a little, your "ought to" self is standing by, ready to help make things right.

Seeing the World in a New Way

Opening yourself up to the possibilities for your life can help you decide to make a life shift, but it will not help you deal with the uncertainty of being on a path that others don't fully understand.

In the months leading up to leaving my job and the year or two after quitting, I struggled to make sense of my journey. When others asked how I was doing, I felt compelled to give them proof that I had a plan and knew what I was doing. It was not until I found the philosopher

Agnes Callard's idea of an aspirational journey that I started to be more comfortable not knowing where I was headed.

Callard defines aspiration as the slow process of "trying on the values that we hope one day to possess."[69] This is in contrast to an ambitious journey where we already know what we value. For example, someone who wants to make a lot of money already values money. They don't need to learn why they want it along the way. An aspirational journey is more ambiguous, and it is harder to predict what sort of values we will adopt along the way.

When we reflect, we find many examples of aspirational journeys in our lives. One example in my life is my love of basketball. When I was younger, I was obsessed with it. I played the sport, watched it, collected trading cards, and read books about the history of the game. I came to understand what I loved and valued about basketball only by continuing to stay interested. Now, when I watch a game and see an incredible play, it moves me in a way that I can't quite articulate. To casual fans, this beauty remains hidden. I've never had any sort of outcome in mind with my love of basketball. Instead, it's been a constant decision to continue to learn and stay engaged with the sport.

This journey contrasts with my pure ambition in college. I took classes with the sole intention of getting the best grade possible. I did not change radically as a person because nothing was at stake. I already valued good grades, which were proof to other people that I was succeeding at a certain kind of game. While ambition does not preclude aspiration, Callard argues that ambition "consumes much of an agent's efforts and does not expand his value horizons."[70]

Aspirational pursuits go hand in hand with the pathless path because they can appear incomprehensible to others and even yourself, some-times for years. Callard argues that the aspirant's understanding of the value of their pursuits "is characterized by a distinctive kind of vagueness, one she experiences as defective and in need of remedy."[71]

Learning to exist with this vagueness is vital, especially at the earliest stages of making a change. It's worth it though, because as Callard says, what is really at stake is you are "learning to see the world in a new way."

Find the Others

According to Callard, people on aspirational journeys, or what I call the pathless path, are "characteristically needy people." Because their worldviews are incomplete and evolving, they are dependent on the support of other people.

My family is filled with people who have thrived on the default path. I had many great role models who taught me the value of hard work, discipline, and commitment, but only on one kind of path. In addition, most of my friends were solidly committed to their full-time jobs. When I was starting to think about taking a different path, I had to find inspiration from podcasts and social media where people like Seth Godin, Derek Sivers, and Tim Ferriss exposed me to a broader set of ideas of how to live and work.

The person I was most drawn to, Seth Godin, had built a life around creativity, generosity, and helping others. I didn't know if I could be like Godin, but knowing that someone like him existed made me believe that kind of path was possible. One of the ideas that Seth Godin is known for is his suggestion that people on unconventional paths seek to "find the others." These are the people who give us inspiration that doing things differently is possible and who might even join us on our journey.

It's no surprise then that many people who take unconventional paths often grew up surrounded by people in their families who also took unconventional paths. Chris Donohoe worked in the consulting industry for several years before launching his own coaching business. He had always been inspired by "an entrepreneurial thread" in his family along with their "work for yourself mentality, and I've always had that as part of who I am."[72] For him, quitting to start his own business was natural.

Others find the others in unexpected places. Lydia Lee, who left a sales job in education in Canada, now runs an online coaching business from Bali and Canada. On a trip she took to Malaysia while still working full-time, she met a digital nomad who was running a marketing firm from his laptop: "being able to meet him in real life...made me realize I could work from my laptop."[73] Meeting that person and her small, but powerful realization planted a seed in Lydia's mind. Even though it would be another six months before she quit her job, she knew a different way of living was possible.

While Lydia happened upon this person by chance and I found people through social media, I suggest people take a more active approach to find what I call "path experts." These are people ahead of you on a path you might be interested in taking. It could be someone who left a job like yours or someone exploring a way of living that fascinates you. Nine times out of ten these people will be enthusiastic about connecting with you because they are still searching for people to learn from on their own journey.

I like to joke that Seth Godin was my only friend on the path before I quit my job. I had read several of his books and devoured all of his podcasts. In today's world, we are lucky to have an abundance of people sharing their stories with us. However, this kind of digital inspiration is often only helpful at the beginning of the journey. Ultimately, you need to find people who are open to a deeper friendship and willing to spend meaningful time together.

I was lucky to stumble upon a few people on the pathless path who would become these kinds of friends at a conference I attended only a few months after quitting my job. I met Noel Boyland, who left a promising consulting career in his early 40s after a health crisis. He's since become the mentor and friend I reach out to when I'm struggling and need a dose of courage. I also met Nita Baum, a consultant, coach, and founder of a talent collective who led a workshop during the conference. In our first conversation, she seemed to know everything about me without needing to ask. When you meet others on a similar path, there is an instant bond and a deep sense of knowing about the challenges you are both going through. You can smile in a way that says, "I know, I know," skip the "what do you do?" question, and start a deeper conversation.

On the pathless path, people like this are essential. You might find them in your family like Chris, while traveling like Lydia, or at a conference like I did. These relationships offer a space where you don't need to have good answers for what you are doing or what comes next. Two "characteristically needy people," as Callard describes them, isn't a recipe for disaster. In my experience, it's usually an opportunity for a beautiful friendship.

On my previous path, there was a hidden cost to my success. The consistent financial rewards helped me live a smooth existence, needing to rely less on others the more I succeeded. In some circles, this is celebrated as the ultimate aim of life, but for me it led to a certain emptiness that I didn't fully understand until I found myself on a path that forced me to find the others.

Tame Your Fears

You can leave the default path before facing your fears, but the pathless path forces you to reckon with them no matter what. I've come to see this as a benefit and I've shifted from someone that kept my fears buried beneath the surface to being aware of my fears and seeing them as tiny but manageable existential crises that are an inevitable part of an uncertain journey.

Although people considering the option of leaving the default path can list hundreds of things that might go wrong, they struggle to talk about the fears behind those risks. In hundreds of conversations with people, I've found that these fears fall into one of the following five areas:

1. Success: "What if I'm not good enough?"
2. Money: "What happens if I go broke?"
3. Health: "What if I get sick?"
4. Belonging: "Will I still be loved?"
5. Happiness: "What if I am not happy?"

During my first few years of self-employment, these fears overwhelmed me, but Tim Ferriss' "fear setting" reflection exercise helped me reframe them and see fear in a completely new way.[74]

The exercise has six steps. The first four are straightforward:

1. Write down the change you are making.
2. List the worst possible outcomes.
3. Identify actions you could take to mitigate those outcomes.
4. List some steps or actions you might take to get back to where you are today.

Writing about fears has helped me transform abstract worries into concrete issues. When I wrote that I was afraid of going broke after I quit my job, I realized that there were fifty different things I could do to make money.

However, some fear-related problems cannot be solved. The authors of *Designing Your Life* offer a helpful reframe, calling these issues "gravity problems" which are part of life "...but, like gravity, it's not a problem that can be solved."[75] This phrase helps me sit with my discomfort when I worry about my health. Due to lingering health issues, I sometimes go long stretches with very little energy. Reminding myself that this is a fact of life, like gravity, helps me accept the uncertainties of life and the pathless path.

The final two questions of Ferriss' exercise are the most powerful:

1. What could be some benefits of an attempt or partial success?
2. What is the cost of inaction in three months, 12 months, and in a few years?

This shifts the focus from the future, which is inherently uncertain, to the present, which helps us see our tendency to overestimate future costs and underestimate costs related to the status quo.

Bronnie Ware has taken care of many elderly people in the final stages of their lives. In a blog post titled, "Five Regrets of The Dying," one of the most viewed online posts, she shared her reflections. The most common regret? Not staying "true to themselves" in their lives and focusing too much on what others expected of them.

The reason articles like this get so much attention is because they get to the heart of what matters to many people, how we spend our lives. Reflections from people at the end of their lives often share similar sentiments, yet very few people know to directly apply it to their lives. The pathless path, however, offers a unique invitation to grapple with our insecurities. If we can accept the invitation, we can continue to ask and then hopefully answer questions about what we really want.

Will They Still Love You?

I have talked with hundreds of people considering a change in their relationship to work or pursuing an alternative path, and one question consistently gets to the heart of their fears: "will the people in your life love you less if you do this?" It's a terrifying question, but worth considering because many people will override their own desires to meet the perceived expectations of others, such as a spouse or parent.

In my first year of self-employment, I knew I wanted to stay on my path, but lacking Callard's language of an aspirational journey, I didn't know how to make any sort of compelling case for why this was true. I shied away from criticism and questions from others, fearful that they would throw me into self-doubt. To protect myself, I overcorrected and developed something my friend Visakan Veerasamy calls "preemptive defensiveness." I saw myself in opposition to the world, seeing the simplest question as an attack on everything I stood for.

After my month-long trip to Asia and experiencing the possibility of working remotely, I had decided to move there for several months that fall. Yet, I hid this from my parents for more than two months despite putting in motion a plan to end my lease, sell most of my stuff, and return to Asia. In fact, they didn't even find out from me, they heard it from my cousin. I was too scared of having the conversation.

A month before I left, I attended a wedding with my family and eventually faced the inevitable questions. At the hotel, everyone started asking: Why was I moving to Taiwan? Wasn't I worried about healthcare? Would I ever have a "real job" again? Didn't I want a family at some point? Why was I doing this? What was my long-term plan?

I felt under attack and that I had disappointed the people that mattered most. My parents had sacrificed so much for me and I felt selfish. Now I know they were coming from a place of love and concern and didn't want to see me suffer. But then, instead of sharing my own fear and uncertainty, I tried to convince them that my evolving vision of the pathless path was the best approach to life.

Unfortunately, the pathless path is an aspirational path and can never be fully explained, as Callard tells us, so attempts to convince people that you are moving in the right direction can be futile. People who value comfort and security often cannot understand why anyone would willingly pursue a path that increases discomfort and uncertainty.

This path offers profound personal growth, but its benefits often remain invisible to others. When you are on such a path, you are hyper-aware of this disconnect, and this can cause a lot of distress. A friend, Amy McMillen, left her finance job after only a year in the workforce to travel and write and recalls the questions that raced through her mind at the time: "What will people think of me? I don't even know what to think of me. Am I being completely irresponsible? Do my parents think I'm a failure? Are my friends as supportive as they seem, or do they think I've gone off the deep end?"[76]

But thinking through such questions can be helpful. In particular, I've found the question, "will the people in your life love you less?" powerful because it addresses the scariest and deepest issues. I didn't want to disappoint my parents. I desperately wanted to convince them that I was doing the right thing. However, had I understood that I feared losing their love, I would have realized that the wiser response would have been to open up my heart and be vulnerable.

At peak uncertainty, I was about to step fully onto the pathless path when I headed halfway around the world to Taiwan. I brought several questions with me. I knew there might not be answers, but I sensed that there was something to be found.

II

The Pathless Path

7

Wisdom of the Pathless Path

August 31st, 2018 (My Newsletter) - *In seven days, I'll be boarding a flight to Taipei to begin a chapter in my life of living and working nomadically. As I've simplified my life and embraced minimalism, I noticed that I have had more time and have been in less of a rush to "do things," giving me the chance to take routes that don't make sense, go for random walks through the city and make time to have conversations I wouldn't otherwise have. I feel so lucky and as I make the shift to Taipei, it seems much less a "vacation" or "trip" and much more an extension of an increased appreciation for life and the people in it.*

* * *

The Life-Changing Magic of Non-Doing

I rolled out of my twin bed and made my way into the living room in the small Airbnb apartment I had booked for my first couple of months in Taipei. It was the fall of 2018 and I had just moved across the globe. I started the coffeemaker and thought about my day and my week. I realized that there was nothing to do.

Technically I was a self-employed freelancer, but I didn't yet have any clients. I had intentions of becoming what people refer to as a "digital nomad," being able to work from anywhere in the world, but didn't know how I would turn that into reality. I was also 33 years old, single, and had recently declared to my friends that I was giving up on dating and shifting to the "cool uncle" phase of my life.

But just a year later I would be planning a tiny wedding, figuring out how to grow the business I created, realizing that writing was an essential part of my journey, and most of all, trying to make sense of my new, deep appreciation for life. Rebecca Solnit supplies the words I didn't have at the time:

> *That thing the nature of which is totally unknown to you is usually what you need to find, and finding it is a matter of getting lost.*[77]

When I arrived in Taipei, I was lost in both the story of my life and in this new place where I couldn't read the signs or speak the language. Yet I also felt I was exactly where I was supposed to be, my days filled with lightness and ease.

This feeling contrasted with the daily tension and low-grade anxiety that I had experienced in New York and Boston over the previous ten years. In Taipei, that feeling evaporated and I started to experience a lighthearted playfulness that had remained dormant since I had wandered in the woods as a kid.

There's a phrase in Chinese, "wu wei," that describes how I felt. In English, its translation is "non-doing," but not in the sense of doing nothing. Non-doing is not about escaping anything or being lazy but instead refers to a deep level of connectedness with the world. The Chinese philosopher Lao Tzu wrote about this more than 2,500 years ago in the Tao Te Ching: "Less and less do you need to force things until finally you arrive at non-action. When nothing is done, nothing is left undone. True mastery can be gained by letting things go their own way. It can't be gained by interfering."[78]

More recently, John Steinbeck channeled this sentiment in a letter to his son, telling him, "If it is right, it happens—The main thing is not to hurry. Nothing good gets away."[79]

In that first month in Taipei, I had stripped down my life to the bare minimum. I had few possessions, was releasing my grip on the future, and was opening myself up to the unknown. I spent these days shifting back and forth between the dizziness of feeling lost and the certainty that I was exactly where I was supposed to be.

Then an invitation to commit to the pathless path showed up.

My first date with Angie was at a tea house in Taipei. She would later tell me that she didn't have high hopes. My dating app profile highlighted my past employers and my graduate school experience. She expected a world-class hoop-jumper. When she shared her frustration with her corporate career and said she'd rather spend her time reading, learning, and exploring the world, she thought I'd be disappointed. But she was wrong. I was falling in love.

On subsequent dates, including bike rides along the river, reading in the park, exploring night markets, and hiking, I discovered someone else who was asking the deeper questions and was willing to embrace uncertainty over doing what was expected. In other words, I had found someone fully embracing their own pathless path.

It's a cliché to say that we find things exactly when we least expect them, but that's exactly what happened to me. For years I had wanted to find someone to be able to "settle down" with. But I was looking for someone within the context of the default path, a script of how life should be rather than what I really wanted. I now agree with Joseph Campbell, who through his study of the human experience through our ancestors' stories, concluded that "We must let go of the life we have planned, so as to accept the one that is waiting for us."[80]

So I might add to Steinbeck's advice: **nothing good gets away, as long as you create the space to let it emerge**.

Living in a world with infinite distractions and interesting goals can make it impossible to stop moving forward. Yet more than ever this is exactly what we crave, and in those first few months in Taipei, I started to see the wisdom in embracing a state of non-doing. For most of my life, I had paired the idea of doing nothing with laziness. Living in another country enabled me to see that this was a very American way of seeing the world. In Taiwan, I was able to embrace a state of doing nothing that was not filled with anxiety and tension, but reflective and open. The possibilities that started to emerge at this time have changed my life. After more than three decades of constantly planning for the future, I was able to start living in the present.

Give Me a Break

The incommunicable trees begin to persuade us to live with them, and quit our life of solemn trifles. – Ralph Waldo Emerson

On his honeymoon, Mohit Satyanand, a successful corporate manager, turned to his wife and asked, "do we need to go back?" They decided not to. Instead, they moved to a small stone cottage in the Kumaon region of India and spent the next six years as he recounted, "in our garden in the forest, watching the peaches grow, and our son toddle." 81

When they returned to the city to send their son to school, Mohit didn't want to return to full-time employment. Although his friends pushed him to get a "real job," his taste of a different life convinced him to continue on the pathless path. He got by on part-time assignments that "paid a fraction of a full-time wage for someone of my age and training," but it was enough.

I read Mohit's story while in Taiwan heading in a similar direction, and I started to wonder if taking a break from work and embracing states of non-doing were effective ways to improve life satisfaction. I was starting to realize a profound and positive shift in how I was thinking about my life and wondered if others had similar results. I reached out to people who had taken such breaks and found that most people credited these breaks from work as one of the most important things in helping them see the possibilities in their life. I also started to notice that many of the shifts that people experienced were somewhat predictable. Four stand out:

First, people become aware of their own suffering. Often we don't notice our drift into a state of low-grade anxiety until we step away from what causes it, as I noticed the first day after I quit my job and realized I was burned out. After my friend, Kevin Jurczyk, took a planned sabbatical, he shared with me, "I used to think 'this job isn't so bad, I make enough money to make it worth it.' Then you get a breath of freedom and realize, no, it may have been worth it at one point, but not anymore."[82]

Similar frustrations with work inspired Jacqueline Jensen, a successful tech founder, to create a "structured sabbatical" to untangle her identity from her work. She asked herself, "What if I took work … working for a paycheck, what if I took that out of the center of my life, what would my life look like?" It was difficult, she says, "to untangle myself from all the things I get from work – the validation, the excitement." [83] However, a month into her break she felt lighter and had a clearer view of what she wanted from work and life.

Second, curiosity re-emerges. When people have time, they try new activities, revisit old hobbies, explore childhood curiosities, and start volunteering and connecting with people in their community. Edward, a friend and a doctor who has taken several sabbaticals, reflected that "new ideas often pop up and old topics of interest float back into my consciousness. I find myself writing notes and thinking more freely. This is the creative process, liberated by the neocortex now that the mind isn't wholly occupied by the strain of everyday sustenance, the rat race, and the grind."[84]

Third, people often desire to continue their "non-work" journey. Lenny Rachitsky, who took a sabbatical after a long career in product management, thought he would return to work, "…but by the end of the break, it was crystal clear to me that I was ready to move on to a new adventure." Several weeks into his sabbatical, he stopped checking his email: "My heart was no longer in the work. I didn't yet know what I wanted to do next, but I knew it was time to shake things up."[85]

Fourth, people write. When Alex Pang took a sabbatical after working in academia and the tech industry, he started to look at life differently, thinking, "maybe we had this idea about the relationship between working hours and productivity backward."[86] Based on that question alone, he spent the next several years writing and publishing several books about how rest and shorter workweeks might improve our lives.

Mohit, Kevin, Jacqueline, Edward, Lenny, Alex, and I were all surprised by how different life feels when it is not structured around work. We also became aware that our previous paths had kept the possibilities for our lives hidden, and in a short time, we started to recapture a youthful energy, one that enabled us all to take bold steps towards different kinds of lives.

Waiting for Retirement

The more we associate experience with cash value, the more we think that money is what we need to live. And the more we associate money with life, the more we convince ourselves that we're too poor to buy our freedom. – Rolf Potts

One of the major barriers to taking a break is believing we have to wait for retirement.

Retirement was introduced in the late 1800s in Germany to provide support for the small number of people who survived to the age of 70 and could no longer work. Now people live longer and are healthier, so retirement is no longer rare, and in some countries, people are projected to spend up to one-third of their life retired. This has led to enormous expectations that this period of one's life will be happy, peaceful, and enjoyable. Part of this is driven by financial firms, which spend millions on advertising campaigns showing happy elderly people smiling as they walk through beautiful meadows. The message? Work hard and invest until you reach the "magical number." Then you can stop and smell the roses.

This version of retirement is a core part of the default path and while it still works for some, the number of people who report being satisfied with retirement in an ongoing survey in the United States has been steadily falling for twenty years.[87] Why might this be? Part of it is that when people stop working, they struggle to replace the meaning and joy they got from their work. I've talked with many people in their 60s and 70s who actively reject the idea that they should stop working. While they often don't have full-time jobs, they enjoy working part-time, volunteering, learning new things, or finding other ways to contribute.

While the traditional idea of retirement is motivating for many, others might benefit from thinking about it from the perspective of the pathless path. On the pathless path, retirement is neither a destination nor a financial calculation, but a continuation of a life well-lived. This shifts attention from focusing on saving for the future to understanding how you want to live in the present.

The best approach I've found for figuring out how I want to live is Tim Ferriss' idea of "mini-retirements," which he introduced in his book, *The Four-Hour Workweek*. He got the idea after realizing that he disliked typical vacations where you pack as much as possible into one or two weeks. After getting burned out on a short trip, he asked himself the question, "Why not take the usual 20–30-year retirement and redistribute it throughout life instead of saving it all for the end?"[88]

With this mindset, he designed his own mini-retirements, trips of "one to six months" where he would test out living in different ways. He described these as an "anti-vacation" and "though it can be relaxing, the mini-retirement is not an escape from your life but a reexamination of it—the creation of a blank slate."[89] While designing these breaks into his life he asked himself three questions:

1. How do your decisions change if retirement isn't an option?
2. What if you could use a mini-retirement to sample your future plans now?
3. Is it really necessary to commit fully to work to live like a millionaire?

The power of these questions is that they force you to be creative and experimental. For me, I've found that this makes life more fun. As I've lived in different places around the world and focused on different kinds of work, I've created mini-experiments that help me learn more about how I want to live my life.

I try to think about time in blocks of one to three months and within each block, I pick one or two things I want to prioritize and test. It might be living in a different type of place, working on new projects, traveling, or learning something new. My goal is to test my beliefs to get a better understanding of what really makes my life better. Many people say things to me like "I could never live like you do!" All I can think, however, is "have you tested that?"

The spirit of the mini-retirement is not about escaping work. It is about testing different circumstances to see if you want to double down on them or change directions. When I started writing this book, I was studying Chinese thirty hours per week and running my online business. It was intense. It's not something I want to do year-round, but these intense periods of learning, creativity, and work followed by periods of rest provide a sustainable and energizing way to stay on this path over the long term. This kind of variability is hard to design into your life on the default path. On the pathless path not only is it possible, but it can be one of the most rewarding benefits.

This kind of experimenting can be time-consuming, but for me, it's worth it. On my previous path, I was more than on my way to a magical retirement number but was also making great progress in undermining the spontaneity, creativity, and energy that would enable me to enjoy life once I got there. For me, testing out different ways of structuring my life now is a win-win proposition. I'm lowering the odds that I'll be unhappy in the future all while crafting a life I'm more and more excited to keep living.

These experiences have given me an alternative to the traditional retirement story. While I'm still saving for retirement, I'm not putting all my faith in reaching certain financial milestones as the most important thing. I'm much more focused on spending time and money now to experiment with different modes of living such that when I reach the latter stages of my life, I won't be making a dramatic shift in life priorities, but continuing on the pathless path.

Have Fun on the Journey

Even though the pathless path does not lead to a specific destination, there may be what Venkatesh Rao, a writer, and consultant, calls "fixed points." A fixed point is a non-negotiable goal that you plan to achieve, no matter what. These fixed points are often a product of our unique cultural scripts. For example, in the United States, as Rao says, the "American Dream" story is based on "the standard fixed point of homeownership. As in, 'no matter what happens in the future, I'll be a homeowner."[90]

We all have fixed points that we aim towards in our lives. Home-ownership is one of the most popular, but others include paying for children's college expenses, becoming an executive or partner, founding a company, or reaching a certain net worth.

The problem with these default fixed points is that they are culturally derived rather than a product of our unique motivations and desires. Over time, this means they can become detached from what is possible or reasonable. For example, in Taipei, people in the previous generation were able to purchase property with only a couple of years of savings from an average job. Now Taipei is home to one of the highest price-to-rent ratios in the world, and this same goal can take more than twenty years and for many, it is simply impossible. While the economic situation has changed radically, many young people orient their lives towards this same goal.

Rao argues that the answer is not to abandon goals altogether but to take them more seriously and to put more thought into identifying unique fixed points, ones that align with the things that bring us alive.

In his book, *On Liberty*, published in 1859, John Stuart Mill was giving similar advice, arguing that societies need people to embrace their individuality and perform "experiments in living." He argued that such experiments are vital to the pursuit of knowledge and that cultures only learn and evolve when original approaches to living are discovered. Mill wanted people to act on their inspiration because "the worth of different modes of life should be proved practically when anyone thinks fit to try them."[91] By choosing a unique and personal fixed point, in Mill's view, you are not only raising the odds of finding a path worth staying on, but you are also serving an important role in pushing culture forward.

Mill argued that conventional ways of living tend to "degenerate into the mechanical" and that if societal norms are too strong or rigid, original thinkers who would otherwise experiment will be stifled. He argues that trying to constrain these people is also not worth doing because they already struggle, "fitting themselves, without hurtful compression, into any of the small number of molds which society provides."[92]

Technology and increased prosperity make this the best time in our history for our own "experiments in living." Yet Mill, who was frustrated in his time with how many people seemed "satisfied with the ways of mankind as they now are," might be surprised at how much shame is still associated with taking a different path.

Embracing a unique fixed point can be an on-ramp to the pathless path. For example, when I was still at my last full-time job, I stopped setting an alarm clock in order to prioritize my health and sleep. I designed my life around that fixed point and did my best to lower the odds that it would lead to challenges at work. Right now, I'm orienting my work around taking every seventh week off from work no matter what. This was inspired by tech entrepreneur Sean McCabe, who adopted the policy for himself and eventually, his entire company.[93]

The fixed points along the default path are not inherently bad, but they do tend to push people towards doing what others do. This can be a good starting point, but if you lean into your own unique psychology, interests, and sense of humor, your journey will be a little more fun and much more meaningful.

In addition, once you are on the pathless path, defining your own constraints and fixed points is not a choice, it's essential to thriving on your journey.

Reimagine Money

The secret to doing good research is always to be a little under-employed. You waste years by not being able to waste hours. — Amos Tversky

When everyone you know builds their lives around a steady paycheck, it is easy to lose track of what we give up for that paycheck and forget that for most of history this was not a normal state of affairs.

When young people excitedly signed up to work for large organizations after World War II, their parents were stunned. They couldn't understand why their children would enthusiastically choose lives characterized by what they saw as containing far too much conformity. William Whyte, wrote about this shift in his book *The Organization Man*, published in 1956. He shared a snippet of writing from a young man typical of the era: "What distinguishes the comfortable young men of today from the uncomfortable young men of the last hundred years...is that for once the younger generation is not in revolt against anything...We don't want to rebel against our elders.[94]

The organizations that these young people joined offered predictable incomes and, most of all, predictable lives. Whyte saw this as a dramatic shift from the past because these organizations offered something that previous generations did not have, a safe haven from the real world, noting that "come graduation, they do not go outside to a hostile world; they transfer."[95]

Because I belong to the third generation of this tradition, I didn't have people around me to tell me how life without a paycheck would feel. When I left my job, I expected that working on my own would be challenging, but I did not expect my entire relationship to money and its role in my life to change.

When I quit, my mindset shifted immediately and I looked at every monetary transaction with the intensity of a financial auditor. I used Mint.com to audit my spending and was shocked that I had been spending nearly $6,000 per month living in New York City. While this was less than I earned, it felt high. After factoring in taxes, I was spending close to $100,000 per year for a life I considered "frugal." This realization embarrassed me, but this story of frugality was easy to believe in a city where there are always people that spend more.

No underlying logic justified my spending and a lot of it could be classified under what writer Thomas J. Bevan calls a "misery tax." This is the spending an unhappy worker allocates to things that "keep you going and keep you functioning in the job."[96] For me, it was a mixture of alcohol, expensive food, and vacations, and as the amount inched up during my career, I started to believe that my spending was the reason I was working.

When I quit, this kind of spending stopped immediately, and I was surprised at how little I missed it. I've since found guidance to reframe how I think about money from Ramit Sethi, an entrepreneur who helps people with personal finances. He asks a great question: "What is your rich life?" The purpose of this question is to stop you from looking at money as an accountant and looking at it as something that might help you live your ideal life. Over time, I've found a clear answer: having ownership of my time enriches my life.

Knowing this inspired me to look for other ways to cut my spending since it would extend the time I could spend on my path without running out of money. When I landed my first real freelance project in Boston, this was what inspired me to sublet my New York apartment, find a cheaper one in Boston, and move there almost immediately. When I added up rent savings, cheaper Chipotle bowls, and the lower tax rate, I was able to lower my spending by about $3,000 per month.

With money coming in and a lower cost of living, my financial insecurity decreased, leading to a chain reaction in my understanding of work. If I wasn't working for money, why was I working? When we work full-time, employers are paying for our dedication and commitment to the job as a central part of our life. When I became self-employed, I was disoriented because the people paying me for the projects didn't care when and how much I worked. They just wanted their problems solved. It was up to me to figure out how to spend my time.

Working on my own, I had infinite degrees of freedom to shape what I worked on, who I worked with, and how much I worked. When people on the pathless path first discover this possibility, it can be jarring. Opting out of work and opting in to other aspects of your life can create questions about who you used to be. It feels weird at first, but over time, you start to change what you value. As I unlocked more time for creative projects, travel with my family, time with my grandmother, and time for learning, I was finally doing the things I claimed to care about.

No amount of money can buy the peace of mind that comes with finding a path that you want to stay on. Once we know, as Vicky Robin argues in her book *Your Money or Your Life*, that "money is something we choose to trade our life energy for," it is nearly impossible to give up your time for money without thinking deeply about the trade-offs.[97]

Have a Little Faith

Belief clings, but faith lets go. – Alan Watts

I was lying on Angie's bed in Taipei, listening to the music playing at the mall just outside her window. She knew that I planned to leave Taiwan and head to Vietnam. In the two months since we had met, however, it had become clear that I wanted to commit to this relationship. Angie had decided to embark on her own pathless path by leaving her corporate job and joining a local gym as a fitness trainer. Before starting, she planned to travel to Thailand for a month. She thought I was going to leave Taiwan and continue exploring the world, which is why I'm still impressed that she asked me so directly, "so… what are your plans for December?"

We had been inseparable. Wandering around Taipei, going to night markets, reading in the park, and having deep conversations about life. It was beautiful. Whenever you are beginning a new relationship, it's easy to fast-forward to the future. Yet I tried to hold back. For most of my life, I had followed a script about how life should be, always trying to choreograph my future. Now I was embracing the pathless path and it was freeing.

On our second date, we rode bikes along the river in Taipei, making our way slowly down the path. We talked about our families, our desires, our fears, and our aspirations. I had felt so alone in the previous year, not able to fully share what I was feeling, and now I was talking to someone who was not only willing to listen but who also seemed to speak the same language.

So I didn't need to hesitate when I answered her question: "I am coming with you to Thailand."

I was guided by faith.

Having faith is admitting that you don't have all the answers for what comes next. Another phrase I've found useful to describe this state of mind is what the spiritual teacher Tara Brach calls "radical acceptance," which she says "is the willingness to experience ourselves and our lives as it is."

Faith is an essential part of the pathless path and many people mention it when talking about embarking on an uncertain path. This was the case for Michael McBride, who decided to leave his job after some of his history-related videos went viral on TikTok. He put it simply, "when I left my job, I took a leap of faith."[98]

Many people I talk to are convinced that the formula for living on their own terms is saving up enough money. I wish they knew what I know: the longer we spend on a path that isn't ours, the longer it takes to move towards a path that is. Money might help pay for therapy, time off, and healing retreats, but it won't help you come to a place where you really trust and know that everything will be okay.

Having faith does not mean being worry-free. I still worry about money, success, belonging, and whether I can keep this journey going. However, I'm able to recognize that the right response is not to restructure my life to make these worries disappear. It's to develop a capacity to sit with those anxieties, focus on what I can control, and to open myself up to the world. As the spiritual teacher Sharon Salzberg has written, "whatever takes us to our edge, to our outer limits, leads us to the heart of life's mystery, and there we find faith."[99] This is the essence of the pathless path, and the only way to develop room for faith in your life is to do exactly as Salzberg says, explore the limits and step into the possibilities for our life. The fact that the next steps are unknown to us is exactly the point.

This is how I knew that the only answer to Angie's question was that I was coming with her to Thailand. On that trip, we made a deeper commitment to each other, and I decided to return to Taiwan indefinitely to support her as she embarked on the next chapter of her journey. I had gone months without a stable income at this point and I didn't know if I would be able to figure out how to make money living abroad. But that didn't seem important at the time. I had faith. I didn't know what was going to happen next, but I had a hunch it was going to be okay.

8

Redefine Success

People have the notion of saving the world by shifting things around, changing the rules, and who's on top, and so forth. No, no! Any world is a valid world if it's alive. The thing to do is to bring life to it, and the only way to do that is to find in your own case where the life is and become alive yourself. – Joseph Campbell

The Second Chapter of Success

In 2019, Gallup surveyed Americans about success. In response to the question, "How do you personally define success?", 97% agreed with the following statement: *A person is successful if they have followed their own interests and talents to become the best they can be at what they care about most.* In response to the question, "How do you think others define success?", only 8% gave the same answer. Instead, 92% felt that other people defined success as follows: *A person is successful if they are rich, have a high-profile career, or are well-known.*[100]

Why the disconnect between how people define success and how we think others define it? Just as when we talk about taking leaps and picking life paths, we simplify the messiness of human nature down to simple stories. When we talk about our goals, we disguise our intentions, especially if we think they demonstrate greed, envy, or pride. We tell only the stories that we think will be seen as acceptable. Everyone knows that we do this, but the result is costly. No one has a clue about others' motivations and we all end up like contestants on *The Bachelor,* convincing ourselves that everyone is striving for success for "the wrong reasons."

Young people pay the highest costs here because they have not yet fully experienced the ups and downs of their own paths and don't have a good understanding of how others are making decisions years ahead of them. They default to "the heuristic of respecting the people who other people respect," as doctor and writer Scott Alexander has noted. In today's world, he says, the most attention and respect goes to people with money, fame, degrees, and power.[101]

In college, I dreamed of working in consulting and getting an MBA from a top-ranked school. I remember looking at the salary reports of graduates from these programs and knowing with every bone in my body that a six-figure salary was what I wanted. At the age of 27, I had miraculously achieved this goal and because I felt so grateful, I hid the fact that I was feeling increasingly lost. The more people I've talked to over the years, the more I've realized that my case is closer to the norm and the people that are on the path they are meant to be on are more the exception than the rule.

Many people realize that they are on the wrong path after achieving impressive milestones. This is what happened to Kevin Durant, a professional basketball player. In 2015, he left his team after nine years to join the best team in the league. In the NBA, players like Durant are judged in part based on whether their team wins a championship. His former team had not. Some players are mocked mercilessly, even after they retire, for failing to achieve this goal. As a result, young players like Durant change teams much more than in the past, doing everything in their power to increase their odds of winning.

The flaw, as Agnes Callard might tell us, is that Durant already knew what he valued and thus, no larger transformation was at stake. It won't surprise us then to find that twelve months later when his team won the championship he was not satisfied. His friend Steve Nash reflected on Durant's confusing emotions that summer: "He didn't have a great summer...He was searching for what it all meant. He thought a championship would change everything and found out it doesn't. He was not fulfilled."[102]

Many people face such a feeling when they finally land a job, a promotion, or even find themselves at a certain phase of life they always desired. As author Ryan Holiday wrote, "You know deep down that accomplishing things won't make you happy, but I think I always fantasized that it would at least feel really good. I was so wrong. Hitting #1 for the first time as an author felt like...nothing. Being a 'millionaire'...nothing. It's a trick of evolution that drives us, and no one is immune from making this mistake."[103] This is what Harvard professor Dr. Ben-Shahar calls the arrival fallacy, the idea that when we reach a certain milestone we will reach a state of lasting happiness.[104]

When we realize that this isn't the case, we find ourselves feeling empty, and the easiest way to deal with this is to ignore the feeling and ratchet up the goal. More money, a bigger house, a new car, a higher salary, an executive position at a company, or a larger retirement nest egg. I once asked a partner at my consulting firm about his dream job. He told me he wanted his boss's position. "At the same company?" I asked. "Then what?" He shrugged and moved on to something else. Something tells me that when the partner achieves his goal, he's not going to feel satisfied.

Eleanor Roosevelt once argued that "when you adopt the standards and the values of someone else or a community… you surrender your own integrity. You become, to the extent of your surrender, less of a human being."[105] I learned this slowly, jumping from job to job doing the same thing that Durant was doing, trying to achieve someone else's goals. For years I believed that once I had achieved an imaginary future leadership position, I would then finally be able to be myself. This is an obvious delusion, but one many people tell themselves.

It was incredibly painful for me to realize that if I truly cared about living in a different way, I might need to leave the business world. The journey towards the pathless path often starts at this moment, with a willingness to investigate your disappointment and to wonder if there is a better way of defining success.

The better way is what I call the "second chapter of success" in which you shift your mindset from what you lack to what you have to offer, from ambition to aspiration, and from hoping that joy will result from a specific outcome to experiencing it as a byproduct of your journey.

People are reluctant to flip the page to the second chapter of success because it requires rejecting paths that are not only more accepted but also promise money, respect, and admiration. However, if we are to believe the results of the Gallup survey, where 97% of people said that their personal definition of success included being "the best they can be at what they care about most," most people desire a path that aligns with what matters uniquely to them. The biggest hurdle then is learning as early as possible the lesson that Kevin Durant learned when he reached the heights of success, and that as Henry David Thoreau once reflected, "the life which men praise and regard as successful is but one kind."[106]

The pathless path is a define-your-own-success adventure. In the first couple years, it felt silly to tell people how I defined success: feeling alive, helping people, and meeting my needs. Over time, I realized that the real benefit of this orientation towards success was that I wasn't competing with anyone. This meant that the odds of success were incredibly high and the benefits of staying on the pathless path would only compound and increase over time.

Prestige and "Bad Tests"

My first week at McKinsey did not feel like work. Instead, it felt like I had gained access to the most interesting club in the world. I thought, "How did I pull this off?" Although most people in my life had no idea what McKinsey was, the friends who did were impressed. Economist Adam Smith once wrote that people desire "not only to be loved, but to be lovely."[107] As soon as I landed the job at McKinsey, I felt lovely, drunk on prestige.

Author Kevin Simler defines prestige as "the kind of status we get from doing impressive things or having impressive traits or skills."[108] In some domains, like sports, this works well. Those we pay the most attention to, like Tom Brady or Lebron James, are also the most skilled. In the business world, however, talent is harder to assess and we tend to use proxies like credentials to determine quality and prestige.

This can be a good way for a company to make talent decisions at scale, but it also motivates many people to seek credentials rather than finding work they enjoy. In my first few weeks at McKinsey, a recruiter from Google connected with me to explain a special program that hired consultants from McKinsey after they had spent two years at the company. If I decided to apply, I'd have a good chance of getting hired. This felt weird. Only a few months earlier, I was desperate to work at either of these companies and now, only a few weeks after adding the McKinsey logo to my LinkedIn profile, I was being granted special status in a "prestige economy" that, as the writer Sarah Kendzior argues, places "money over merit, brand over skill."[109]

This kind of status was not something I shied away from, but deep down I knew that the underlying skill I was being rewarded for was my ability to hack the system. Almost everyone who works in these fields understands that passing these "bad tests" is how things work but no one, including me, at first, imagines there is another option.

Paul Graham, the investor and startup mentor, argues that far too many young people believe learning how to hack bad tests is a necessary part of success. In his work with entrepreneurs, he struggles to convince them that they don't need to play these games. He shares a common back-and-forth he has with founders about the factors that lead to success:

> How does one get lots of users? They had all kinds of ideas about that. They needed to do a big launch that would get them 'exposure.' They needed influential people to talk about them. They even knew they needed to launch on a Tuesday, because that's when one gets

the most attention. No, I would explain, that is not how to get lots of users. The way you get lots of users is to make the product really great.[110]

When you've spent your entire life studying for the test and compiling long lists of achievements it can be hard to believe that true success is that simple. In the consulting industry, bad tests were prevalent. While the quality of your work was important, other tests like getting senior partners to like me, taking any work given to me, dressing the right way, and learning to speak in a certain way were much more important in getting promoted, getting a raise, and continuing on an impressive career trajectory.

I don't think I realized how much I hated this until I became self-employed and immediately stopped spending any time hacking tests. With freelancing, I was competing on the quality of my ideas and my ability to do good work for clients. A lot of former consultants who become freelancers are surprised at how much less time it takes to do the same work. This is not because it's any easier. In fact, it's a lot harder without the support of an entire firm's resources. It's just that there are no longer hundreds of different people you need to impress.

Working on my own, I'm no longer in Kendzior's prestige economy where brand is more important than skill. I'm in an indie economy, where over the long-term I'm competing on learning, developing skills, and my reputation. This is a lot harder but also a lot more rewarding. Despite this, it's interesting to see how people map their own understanding of how they think the world works onto my current path. Many people say things like, "you can do this because you worked at McKinsey and went to MIT." They assume that my credentials are what matter most. I wish this were the case! While having impressive credentials can open doors, it hasn't translated into a high income, especially with some of the more creative things I've done like writing or online courses.

It took a long time for me to realize that I was not stuck hacking bad tests for the rest of my life. While I was at MIT, I read William Deresiewicz's essay, "The Disadvantages of An Elite Education." His argument that elite schools often incentivize behaviors that undermine living a meaningful life excited me, but I had no idea what to do about it. People are very aware of the absurdity of much of what you have to do to succeed in different companies and institutions, but still often gaslight themselves by starting off their own complaints with, "I know I should be grateful, but...".

With more possibilities to work independently and become an entrepreneur, I'm here to tell you to take your own doubts seriously and demand better! It is no longer true that to succeed, you need to hack bad tests. I agree with Graham when he says, "It used to be true. In the mid-20th century, when the economy was composed of oligopolies, the only way to the top was by playing their game."[111]

The world is changing and the pathless path is just one way to exit the world of bad tests. As more and more people decide that these tests are silly, we can create new and better games. Ones that aren't optimized for how employers like to see the world, but rather align with how we are motivated to learn and grow through our lives. I think this really matters and I agree with Graham's assessment: "This is not just a lesson for individuals to unlearn, but one for society to unlearn, and we'll be amazed at the energy that's liberated when we do."[112]

Find Your Tribe

The internet has made my new life and career on the pathless path possible. In my last full-time job, I started writing short articles about my thoughts on the future of work. I was writing on my own and not with the permission of my company. This was scary because at my company, only senior executives were encouraged to share their thoughts on social media.

My fears subsided as I started to make friends through writing. After posting one article, I received a message from someone who was a Chief Talent Officer at a company in New York City. He was enthusiastic about my curiosity and proposed we meet up for coffee. We had a lively discussion, the kind that leaves you with more energy than when you arrived. I wanted more of that, which motivated me to keep writing. This also exposed me to a new kind of prestige that I wasn't allergic to – recognition from other people who are passionate about ideas.

Increasingly, the internet is supporting the emergence of many micro-communities that provide people with attention and prestige in unique ways. For example, I participate in an evolving "creator economy" ecosystem that has developed on Twitter, in private groups and online courses, and through real-life meetups. One way to earn prestige in this world is to give generously and share everything you know. People like Nat Eliason, Anne-Laure Le Cunff, Pieter Levels, and Tiago Forte have earned status not only because of their extrinsic success but also their willingness to support others and share in extensive detail how they make money and how they think about their lives.

The concept of prestige is shifting quickly. As our connections to local communities have broken down, we are paying more attention than ever to people who are successful in the traditional sense, through money, status, or fame. But below this flashy surface, many people are seeking out smaller and quieter communities where they can earn prestige in a way that suits their lives.

These communities, many of which have emerged online, have been a welcome companion to me on the pathless path. I've been surprised at how many people across the globe resonate with my story and are searching for a different game to play than hacking the "bad tests" that Paul Graham writes about. Now it's easier than ever to open your computer and opt-in to a community that defines prestige, status, and success in a way that matches how you want to design your life.

The internet does enable negative groups to form, but we pay far too much attention to these communities and not enough to the positive connections and life options made possible all over the world for people who are online. If the default path is the story of the industrial world, then the pathless path is the natural story for a digital-native world in which nothing can stop us from finding others who share our desires, ideas, and questions.

When I took a break from freelancing in the first year of my self-employment journey, I decided to spend more time writing online, launching my podcast, and building an online course. In 2018, this was not an obvious path to success. I worked on those things for more than eighteen months before I made more than $1,000. Why would I keep working on these things? Because I had found a small group of people that saw value in what I was doing and encouraged me to keep going.

It's hard to overstate how powerful this force has been in my life. Seth Godin argues that humans are wired "to become a member in good standing of the tribe" and on the default path this means we will tend to conform.[113] On the pathless path, powered by digital communities, we can surround ourselves with people that inspire us and push us to improve in the ways we care about. The longer I've stayed on this path and the more effort I've put into connecting with people heading in similar directions, the better my life has become.

This is why I'm fond of the advice angel investor Naval Ravikant offers, "play long-term games with long-term people." Ever since making that first friend from my writing, I haven't stopped writing publicly for more than five years, mostly driven by the fact that I continue to meet great people. One example is my friend Saloni Miglani in India, who quit her job and became a remote worker. In a note she sent to me, she told me that "your writing showed me how I could be a happier, calmer, and more creative human being." Little does she know that I learn just as much from her, and others like her every week.

Early on, it was clear that if I continued to share over a long enough period of time, it might radically improve my life. As I'm writing this book, I can say without a doubt that my hunch was correct.

You Are a Bad Egg

In his book *Seeing Like a State*, James Scott argues that "legibility" made modernity possible. By legibility, he means "arranging the population in ways that simplified the classic state functions of taxation, conscription, and prevention of rebellion."[114]

One example of this standardization is Germany's invention of "scientific forestry." By using the output of paper as a measurement for a specific volume of trees, forests could be quantified and trees could be planted to optimize output. This method worked well in the short term, but within a couple of generations, it resulted in costs such as the loss of important local species and soil degradation. It turns out that Mother Nature's approach was wiser than the scientists understood.

This kind of quantification has now been applied to many parts of society. In terms of work, the fundamental organizing unit of the economy is the "job." This is why so much attention is paid to unemployment rates, also called the "jobs numbers." The former academic turned writer and financial advisor Ben Hunt has argued that for most of the 20th century, such standardization was "industrially necessary" and vital to the success of the modern economy, state, and world.[115]

However, he continues, over the last 50 years the need for people to be "legible" and fit into a standard model of work has merely become "industrially preferable." This puts government and institutional leaders in a position where they are incentivized to convince people that following rigid paths in their institutions is the correct path for everyone. Hunt uses the example of the "industrially necessary egg," to make his point. "Good" eggs are those that meet specifications, are perfectly clean, and can legally be sold in a supermarket.

Any farmer knows, however, there are other good eggs, such as the ones from Hunt's farm, which are often dirty, come in various shapes, and don't need to be refrigerated. Many people see these as bad eggs, but Hunt knows the truth, that they are "one of the best things in life."[116]

Hunt's eggs provide a good metaphor for thinking about the pathless path. On the default path, you are automatically a "good egg." On the pathless path, people default to seeing you as a "bad egg." Even if it was never spoken, when I left the default path I felt as if I had immediately crossed an imaginary boundary where I was some sort of rebel that needed to defend my recklessness.

The belief that full-time work is normal, however, doesn't match with reality. In 2013, Gallup found that the global payroll to population rate, or the percentage of people working full-time, to be 26%.[117] If only a quarter of the population has "good egg" jobs, maybe the prevailing story that tells us how we should think about work and the economy is not the best one. At a minimum, we should be a little more suspicious of anyone who seems to think there is one true way of working.

Yet this is the world we live in. This means embracing the pathless path requires grappling with the feeling of being a "bad egg." This often drives people who leave the default path to eagerly embrace new identities that are still recognizable as legible to the "traditional" economy. They gravitate to titles like a startup founder, entrepreneur, freelance consultant, or even the newly emerging "creator."

For example, when Khe Hy first left his job on Wall Street, he shared that his initial plan was, "to become a venture-backed entrepreneur." He wanted to start a company and raise capital from investors. As he reflected later, "it sounds so lame, but to me a big portion of success was other people thinking I was successful."[118]

Embracing a new identity can be a useful way to enter the uncertain world of the pathless path. At a minimum, it gives you an answer when people inevitably start asking about your plans. However, many people quickly realize that they've created the same conditions that they sought to escape. Luckily, Khe figured this out, and before he got started, he said that he "had just enough separation" from his old life that he knew he wanted something much different than founding a company, at least in the first couple years of his journey.

The pathless path is about ignoring the pull of needing to be a "good egg" and learning what truly enables you to thrive. What this really means is developing an appreciation for discomfort. Howard Gray, a consultant and storyteller, and veteran of the pathless path, sees the uncertainty of his path as a positive thing. When his life "stops moving and it calcifies or solidifies, that's a bad thing" and he's on the right track when it's a "formless, evolving thing."[119]

The comfort we feel when we do what is expected keeps us from developing the skills we need to face uncertainty. Noah Lowry, a pitcher for the San Francisco Giants, dedicated his childhood and early adulthood to baseball. But injuries forced him to retire when he was just 26, early for a professional athlete. This experience rocked Lowry's world; he described it as "disorienting and chaotic." Later he recounted, "In a moment, my identity crumbled, who I thought I was, the man my wife thought she had married, fell apart."[120] Lowry had reached the heights of success in his field, but when that was taken away, he realized he did not have the skills needed to embark on a new path.

Chauncey Billups came to the same realization after retiring from professional basketball at the age of 37. Even though his career wasn't shortened by injury as Lowry's was, he was still rattled: "You go from being a very old dude at 37...to being a young dude with no real experience anywhere else. You can become lost."[121]

This reminds me of Rebecca Solnit's insight about getting lost in *A Field*

Guide To Getting Lost. She says that, "losing things is about the familiar falling away," but "getting lost is about the unfamiliar appearing."[122] Billups was losing his career at the same time he was becoming lost, heading in a new direction. If a professional athlete like him was not prepared, even after earning more than $100 million in his career, this tells us that learning how to deal with uncertainty is not a natural thing, or at minimum is something that can't be "solved" with more money.

Part of the promise of being a "good egg" is that we will not feel lost. But the "bad eggs" on the pathless path eventually realize there is wisdom in being lost. This doesn't mean it will be easy. Like Billups, you will sense that you are doing something wrong, or at minimum, don't know what you are doing. Simple questions from others like "what do you do?" will expose your own uncertainty and can feel like a death blow to the soul.

We can weaken the impact of these kinds of questions by knowing that there is no way to avoid being seen as a "bad egg." The only way forward is to eventually get to a point when you realize that, in fact, there are no good eggs or bad eggs at all. The pathless path is about releasing yourself from this way of seeing the world and realizing that the number of career paths worth following is infinite.

As Thoreau once wrote at Walden Pond, "Not till we are lost, in other words, not till we have lost the world, do we begin to find ourselves, and realize where we are and the infinite extent of our relations."[123]

Find Your "Enough"

Are you helping people? Are they happy? Are you happy? Are you profitable? Isn't that enough? – Derek Sivers

Paul Jarvis, a designer and entrepreneur, wrote *Company of One*, which details his efforts to build a sustainable business and life. At many stages along his journey, people urged him to grow his business, hire employees, and earn more money. But at every opportunity, he chose to keep working alone. Over time he built a path that he was excited to stay on and realized that "a large part of choosing your path is figuring out which values will determine your worth." Once he had a good understanding of those values, it was easier for him to decide where to focus.[124]

Coming to this understanding requires a lot of reflection and experimentation, but surprisingly, this is often much easier on the pathless path than the default path. Because I work for myself, I spend zero minutes a year blaming other people for my circumstances. It forces me to take complete ownership of my life and continue to experiment, reflect, and try again. In six months I can experiment with my life in many more ways than I did in the ten years I spent on the default path, allowing me to learn much more quickly.

Over time, you start to understand what matters, and more importantly, when to say "no." To engage with these issues, Jarvis wrote a personal definition of "enough." Notice how detailed it is:

Enough is the antithesis of unchecked growth because growth encourages mindless consumption and enough requires constant questioning and awareness. Enough is when we reach the upper

130

bound of what's required. Enough revenue means our business is profitable and can support however many employees/freelancers we have, even if it's just one person. Enough income means we can live our lives with a bit of financial ease, and put something away for later. Enough means our families are fed, have roofs over their heads and their futures are considered. Enough stuff means we have what we need to live our lives without excess.[125]

Jarvis knows and can articulate what matters to him and he is not afraid to share it. For many in full-time jobs, this kind of reflection can be hard, if not impossible. For example, very few people would ever consider walking into their manager's office in September and declaring, "I've made enough money for this year. See you in January!" Instead, it is easier to accept the economic logic of profit-seeking organizations, that "more is better," and apply it to our own lives.

This approach can work for some, but it drives many towards burnout. Writer Jocelyn Glei, who worked at a startup, noted, "After being at a startup for four years and getting the chance to make tons of cool stuff, I was intoxicated with my own productivity. I got wildly ambitious and decided to 3x my workload, adding multiple massive new projects (of my own devising!) to an already intensive work schedule." It was hard for her to see what was happening because she liked the work so much. However, "by the end of that year, I had produced a ton of incredible things, but I was a burnt-out husk of a person." She calls this her "busyness breakdown." After work she had no energy left to invest in relationships, health, and other things that mattered to her. She realized that when "the way we work today and the way we work tomorrow becomes the status quo," it quickly becomes "the new normal," and that crafting a new approach to living your life becomes really hard. She was incredibly productive, but for her, it was not enough.[126]

As I developed a better relationship with money and stopped acting from a mindset of scarcity and fear, I started to work out my own perspective on "enough":

Enough is knowing that no amount in my bank account will ever satisfy my deepest fears. It's knowing that I have enough friends that would gladly open their door and share a meal if I was ever in need. It's the feeling that I've been able to spend my time over an extended stretch of time working on projects that are meaningful to me, helping people with a spirit of generosity, and having enough space and time in my life to stay energized to keep doing this over the long-term. Enough is seeing a clear opportunity that will increase my earnings in the short-term, but knowing that saying "no" will open me up to things that might be even more valuable in ways that are hard to understand. Enough is knowing that the clothes, fancy meal, or latest gadget will not make me happier, but also that buying such things won't mean I'm going to end up broke. Enough is having meaningful conversations with people that inspire me, people that I love, or people that support me.

On the pathless path, knowing you have enough is what gives you the freedom to say "no" to clear financial opportunities and say "yes" to something that might bring you alive and might even pay off much more over the long term.

When I launched a podcast, people assumed it was a massive project and that I wanted to compete with Gimlet and NPR. They didn't know that I considered it an experiment and wasn't aiming toward monetary success or fame. From this perspective, it made sense to create a podcast cover in 20 minutes in PowerPoint, spend less than an hour editing the audio, and publish without much of a following. There was nothing else to gain because I was operating from the feeling of enough.

If we don't define "enough," we default to *more*, which makes it impossible to understand when to say *no*.

When I wrote this section, I emailed Jarvis and asked him to expand on his "Enough" essay, but I got an automated response, "Please note, this email address is no longer active or monitored."

It seems Jarvis knows when enough is enough.

Beyond Scarcity Mindset

The problem is that our culture has engaged in a Faustian bargain,
in which we trade our genius and artistry for apparent stability.
– Seth Godin

My mother credits the health crisis I faced in my 20s for putting me on my current path. "It changed you," she says.

While I don't think it was the sole reason I left the default path, my illness did change my relationship to uncertainty. While I was sick, I went several months without a paycheck, spent thousands on healthcare, and watched my savings dwindle down to less than three months of living expenses. Three years later, I had saved up five times the amount I had in savings. So the prospect of leaving without an income didn't seem so scary.

Without my health crisis, I probably wouldn't have been so comfortable leaving my job without any clear plan for making money. This seems crazy now, but it didn't occur to me to radically cut my spending until *after* I left my job. A trained consultant and former financial analyst who had spent hundreds of hours building models for companies and I had never bothered to create a detailed model of my own spending. What was I thinking?

This is not how most people approach quitting their job. What I've discovered in conversations is that no matter how much money people have, they will go to enormous lengths to avoid any discomfort related to their financial situation. This is what makes quitting full-time employment seem terrifying and a steady paycheck so addictive.

Economist Daniel Kahneman found that "the importance that people attached to income at age 18 also anticipated their satisfaction with their income as adults."[127] While on the default path, I was always surrounded by people that cared more about money and it was easy to convince myself that I placed very little importance on money. When I quit my job, I realized my assessment was wrong.

Though I had gone several months without a paycheck while sick, the months after leaving my job were a completely different experience. Money went from a background consideration to one of the most important things in my life. I was experiencing what psychologists call, "scarcity mindset."

Some of the first research into this state of mind was done in 1944. Worries about food shortages due to the war led to research about how people react to going without food.[128] Researchers at the University of Minnesota recruited 36 participants for a study that involved long stretches without eating. In addition to the expected biological reactions, the men became obsessed with food. They talked about opening restaurants and switching careers to work in food service, shared recipes, and compared food prices across various newspapers. The researchers concluded that when we feel we lack something, we tend to obsess over it.

When I first left my job I was similarly "starved" of my paycheck. This inspired my cost-cutting move to Boston and drove me to go all-in on finding freelance projects. This calmed the feelings of scarcity for a while but distracted me from getting to the root of my insecurities.

When I moved to Taiwan, I intended to seek out freelancing work but was pulled in by both the magic of non-doing and the excitement of a new relationship. Without money coming in, I shifted my attention to cutting expenses even further. With the assistance of a spending tracking app, I scrutinized every purchase like a seasoned accountant and was able to lower my cost of living to less than $1,000 per month. Again, this lessened the pressure to make money but it kicked a deeper reckoning with my feelings down the road.

When I started to make plans with Angie to stay in Asia, I started to worry about making money again. This led me to accept a freelance project with a small consulting firm. It paid $7,500, which would fund my life for several months, but when I started working on the project, I realized I had talked myself into the project in order to calm my fears rather than as something I was excited to work on. I committed to not making the same mistake again.

American anthropologist Ernest Becker was convinced that most of our actions in life are driven by a fear of death. Behind my money fears was a longing to feel that my life mattered. I suspect this is the same for many, and money is one shortcut we use to "prove" our worth. Yet in my experience, no amount of money ever seems to satisfy. Becker argues that the only way to transcend these existential fears is to live a life that feels heroic. He argues that "if everyone honestly admitted his urge to be a hero it would be a devastating release of truth."[129]

What he means by heroic is less about saving the world and closer to the pathless path: a journey of finding yourself, grappling with your insecurities, and daring to seek out a life that is uniquely yours. Becker argues that prescribed paths of the modern world can trap people into conforming to the expectations of others instead of taking steps to create their own unique path.

On the pathless path, the pressure of conformity is not a major concern, but that does not mean an ideal life will emerge automatically. You need to take steps to create it, and in those months in Asia, I started to realize that I needed to graduate from my role as accountant. Minimizing spending is a useful step in lowering the pressure of making money, but it's not a lifestyle. While it gave me the confidence to make drastic changes without sacrificing my happiness, it kept me in a mindset of scarcity instead of leaning into possibility.

Do I still worry about money? Yes. But now I'm hyper-aware of how my financial insecurities might distract me from efforts that will help me stay energized and motivated on this path. Instead of playing to not lose, I'm playing to win.

Behind our money fears are existential fears, like the fear of death or the fear of not being loved, respected, and admired. These fears are likely not solvable but we can learn to coexist with them. This is also why financial worries can be infinite and people can chase more and more their entire lives. The flip side of this is that if we can learn to coexist with our financial insecurities, we can turn them into a secondary concern. This opens you up to the real secret: the opportunities of the pathless path are infinite too.

9

The Real Work of Your Life

There's so much more to who you are than you know right now.
You are, indeed, something mysterious and someone magnificent.
You hold within you – secreted for safekeeping in your heart –
a great gift for this world. Although you might sometimes feel
like a cog in a huge machine, that you don't really matter in the
great scheme of things, the truth is that you are fully eligible for a
meaningful life, a mystical life, a life of the greatest fulfillment
and service. – Bill Plotkin

Finding Your Conversation

I've been inspired by the poet David Whyte's way of interpreting the
world, which he calls the "conversational nature of reality." He believes
all of us have an ongoing "conversation" with the world. While this
may play in literal conversations with others or ourselves, it can also
be metaphorical. What I've taken it to mean is that we all have things
we are meant to find out about ourselves and the only way to discover
them is to open ourselves up to the world.

One of the best ways to discover your conversation is to start asking questions driven by your curiosity. For me, some of my favorite questions include:

- What matters?
- Why do we work?
- What is the "good life"?
- What holds people back from change?
- How do we find work that brings us alive?

These are not simple, but when I learned to be guided by my curiosity and pay attention, I started noticing that answers would spontaneously emerge as a byproduct of living my life. It's also when you know you've found a "real conversation" which as Whyte describes, "is one that, no matter how slowly, helps you make sense of the world around you."[130]

The conversational nature of reality is most apparent when you are willing to exist at "the frontier" of your current reality. As Whyte reflects, "It's astonishing how much time human beings spend away from that frontier." The default path keeps people from this frontier but the pathless path pushes you towards it. To Whyte, the cost of not moving towards the frontier is profound, as we often risk missing out on a "deeper, broader, and wider possible future that's waiting."[131]

I was first forced towards the edge of my reality the first week after quitting my job. I set out to wander around New York and ended up at a park called the Cloisters, at the literal frontier of New York, a city that I had failed to fully explore in the two and a half years that I had been there. I wandered through the park overlooking the Hudson. I felt lost, but not in a way that I could do anything about. If you had asked me where I was headed, I wouldn't have had an answer. If you suggested I might move to Boston in a few months, I might have believed you. But if you said I'd end up in Asia, married, a little over two years later? I wouldn't have even known what to do with that information. Being at the frontier of your current reality is disorienting. Deep down you might have a sense that you should keep going in a certain direction, but you never know why.

This is what Whyte means when he writes about the conversational nature of reality. It's an acknowledgment that there are deeper forces at play in the world and we are a tiny little part of all that magic. It's about existing within that magic and still daring to ask questions about what matters or where you fit in. Much of my previous life had been scripted into a routine and I spent almost all my time knowing where I was supposed to be. This short-circuited my curiosity for years and kept me from seeing that there was a "conversation" with the world to be had at all.

When you step off the default path, you will be thrust towards the frontier. Almost immediately, clues about your conversation will emerge from what captures your attention and questions will appear that gives you a better understanding of what you're really after. This will be a confusing time. You may feel the urge to tell everyone about your new insights, questions, and curiosities, but this can be a mistake. Your ideas may make others uncomfortable and any doubt, skepticism, or criticism they express could convince you to run away from the frontier.

My own conversation has evolved slowly. At first, it was a solo conversation with broad, ambiguous questions ignited by losing my grandfather and losing my identity during my health crisis. This morphed into a more complex conversation over time, one that involved realizations from my life as well as from other people I was meeting through my writing. These connections were vital to staying at the frontier and exploring. In my favorite essay, "Solitude and Leadership," William Deresiewicz highlights the importance of searching for wisdom in real conversations with close friends:

> *Introspection means talking to yourself, and one of the best ways of talking to yourself is by talking to another person. One other person you can trust, one other person to whom you can unfold your soul. One other person you feel safe enough with to allow you to acknowledge things—to acknowledge things to yourself—that you otherwise can't. Doubts you aren't supposed to have, questions you aren't supposed to ask. Feelings or opinions that would get you laughed at by the group or reprimanded by the authorities.*[132]

While the pathless path is a solo journey, it is important that you have at least one close friend with whom you can have these kinds of intimate conversations. They will help you remain aware of your own emerging conversation with the world.

I've been lucky to find many people willing to have those conversations with me that have helped me be comfortable exploring my own frontier. The benefits of this have been profound. While I don't have perfect answers yet for the questions I keep asking, my conversation has somehow turned into a full life, one filled with people, ideas, curiosities, and work that will keep me engaged for many years to come.

Design for Liking Work

We are always falling in love or quarreling, looking for jobs or fearing to lose them, getting ill and recovering, following public affairs. If we let ourselves, we shall always be waiting for some distraction or other to end before we can really get down to our work. The only people who achieve much are those who want knowledge so badly that they seek it while the conditions are still unfavorable. Favorable conditions never come. – C.S. Lewis

John O'Nolan set a goal for himself to build a $1 million company by the time he turned 30. After several failed attempts, he decided to reevaluate. He realized that if he stuck to this goal, he might achieve it, but he might build a company he didn't want to be part of.

He shifted his approach towards building a business that he wanted to be "stuck with" and revisited an idea that he had sidelined: building a new blogging platform. His idea seemed silly. Everyone used dominant platforms like WordPress or Blogger. Who was he to try to compete in that space? Nevertheless, he decided to go for it and founded a new blogging platform named Ghost.

To ensure that he was taking a long-term approach, John made decisions that differed radically from those that are made in a traditional startup. For example, he wouldn't control the shares and he would not be able to sell the company. In an interview with Ali Abdaal, he said, "I don't own Ghost. I am a trustee of Ghost, which means I can steer it as an owner would, but if I ever get sick of it, I can't sell it. I don't own any shares."[133] This is opposed to how almost everyone in the technology industry operates, but it makes sense if you're planning on sticking with the company you're building.

Instead of optimizing for a future "exit," or a sale of the company, he built a company he wanted to keep working at and all his decisions continue to be based on this goal. As his platform grew, corporations started asking the company to do customized installations for them. John decided he didn't want to deal with these high-maintenance customers and turned them down. Despite this obvious opportunity, Ghost still does not employ a single employee that works with enterprise customers. John learned the same lesson I had in taking the client that had drained my energy. No money is worth it if it undermines your desire to stay on the journey.

Many stumble upon the work they enjoy doing by saying "no" to obvious opportunities. John reflected, "As soon as I let go of this notion of huge success, that's when success started coming to me." I don't think this is a random occurrence. Saying no to something requires that we know what we stand for. When I decided to say no to future freelance projects, I knew that it was time to take my writing, my online business aspirations, and my other ideas seriously.

On the pathless path, the goal is not to find a job, make money, build a business, or achieve any other metric. It's to actively and consciously search for the work that you want to keep doing.

This is one of the most important secrets of the pathless path.

With this approach, it doesn't make sense to chase any financial opportunity if you can't be sure that you will like the work. What does make sense is experimenting with different kinds of work, and once you find something worth doing, working backward to build a life around being able to keep doing it.

It's a shift from the mindset that work sucks towards the idea that you can design a life around liking work. I didn't realize how profound this shift is until I sat down to write this book.

When I first left my job I was running away and wanted to escape. This desire drove me to design my life around flexibility, which I achieved to a remarkable degree. I went from having to be in an office more than 2,000 hours per year to having to spend less than a couple of days each month in any physical location.

Unfortunately, this life was built around freelancing and my heart was never in it. I still enjoy working on some consulting projects, but it's not what drives me. The work that I want to keep doing is writing, sharing stories, helping people, and doing other experiments online. When I started my podcast and blog it felt silly to like this kind of work. Now I know that this is the real work that matters.

Finding work you want to keep doing, says author Stephen Cope, is "the great work of your life." Cope's biggest fear is that he might "die without having lived fully."[134] This impulse drove his curiosity as he sought out wisdom in books, reading upwards of three hours a day. Eventually, he wrote *The Great Work of Your Life* to explore the unique qualities of people who search for the things that bring them alive. His exploration was inspired by a passage he read in the Gospel of Thomas:

> *If you bring forth what is within you, what you bring forth will save you. If you do not bring forth what is within you, what you do not bring forth will destroy you.*[135]

He researched the lives of Susan B. Anthony, Robert Frost, John Keats, Harriet Tubman, and Henry David Thoreau and found that the common trait they shared was seriously attempting to bring forth what was inside of them. This didn't come easy to any of them and they all faced challenges, rejection, and criticism. Yet at every key point in their lives, they either kept looking for what brought them alive or protected their time so that they could work on what mattered. In the words of Thoreau, the game they played and that we should play is to "be resolutely and faithfully what you are."[136]

When I think about the people that "bring forth what is inside of them," I think about my mother. She got a job at my university while I was in my second year, and she quickly became the go-to person not only for solving financial aid problems but, for many of my friends, as someone to talk to. She was a mentor and friend to the students that worked for her. In our extended family, she is the planner who makes sure that everyone comes together. In our small town, she lends a hand when people fall ill, raises money for the needy, and plays an active role in improving the school. In every role she steps into, she finds a way to give all that she has to offer.

However, she also consistently urges me to take a "comfortable state job," no matter how happy I am or how much success I've found on my new path. She's usually half-joking but the suggestion fascinates me. Where does the impulse to find a comfortable job, no matter the personal cost, come from? I think it is partly due to our narrow conception of work as only a full-time job with a salary and benefits. Like Cope, however, I have embraced a broader conception of work and agree with him that the search for work worth doing is the real work and one of the most important pursuits in life.

It's hard to understate how much the narrow conception of work constrains us and this has become obvious to me observing my wife

145

explore various art projects such as watercolor and acrylic painting, drawing and sketching, rock painting, Zentangle, and others. Her work impresses and inspires me. It is work worth doing and it will crush me if she loses her passion for it. Yet when she shares her work, especially with people in the United States, they always suggest that she monetize: "You should offer painting classes!" "Are you going to sell those?" "You could make a lot of money!" The assumption is that making money or finding a way to turn a passion into a job is one of the most important things. While money is important on the pathless path, using it as a filter for finding the work worth doing, especially at first, is a mistake.

More important is the realization that finding something worth doing indefinitely is more powerful and exciting than any type of security, comfort, stability, or respect a job might offer. Fighting for the opportunity to do this work is what matters, whether or not you make money from it in the short term.

I was slow to realize this, but I know it now. The work I get paid for may shift over time, and it may or may not involve the things that I want to keep doing. But what I want to keep doing, such as mentoring young people, writing, teaching, sharing ideas, connecting people, and having meaningful conversations, is worth fighting for.

I am consciously pursuing a life designed around doing work I like and I'm lucky to have someone to look up to like my mother, whose life has embodied this principle, whether she set out to do this on purpose or not. She can find a role or a place for herself in many environments. I struggled to find my place on my previous path, so now I'm taking a different one. I hope I can convince those of you who are like me that searching for work you like and want to keep doing is worthwhile.

Most of all, I yearn for a world where more people can live like my mother.

We Want To Be Useful

Usefulness, whatever form it may take, is the price we should pay for the air we breathe and the food we eat and the privilege of being alive. And it is its own reward, as well, for it is the beginning of happiness, just as self-pity and withdrawal from the battle are the beginning of misery. – Eleanor Roosevelt

According to Robert Kegan, a psychologist at Harvard, we are shifting away from a world where we need to fit in towards one where we must develop the skill of "self-authoring."[137] Instead of looking to external cues to learn how to live, we need to have a coherent internal narrative about why we are living a certain way. This is the ethos of the pathless path and if you don't know or understand your own story, you will struggle.

One of the hardest questions people face when they think of their own story, however, is "what should I do?"

A significant barrier to figuring out what we really want to do is the voice in our head that warns us to stop when we consider or start doing things that are not broadly seen as "normal." Professor and author Brene Brown's clarification of shame and guilt helped me understand what's really going on when we struggle to pay attention to our intuitions and desires. She defines shame as "the intensely painful feeling or experience of believing that we are flawed and therefore unworthy of love and belonging." She believes that most people give too much power to this emotion when making life choices."[138]

She doesn't think we can "solve" shame and suggest that people pay attention to a slightly different emotion, guilt. She defines guilt as "holding something we've done or failed to do up against our values and feeling psychological discomfort."[139] In contrast to shame, guilt is actionable. The disconnect between what we claim to care about and what we do (or don't do) points out what matters to us.

Guilt drives many people to work, and this is a normal reaction to this uncomfortable emotion. Most people want to contribute, help, and engage with the world. However, sometimes this impulse gets hacked by our shame and we follow paths that aren't ours because we feel like the world's love depends on us doing a certain thing. We are afraid that if we step away or make a change, we might be cast out of our family or community. This is one of life's most terrifying feelings and keeps many from making changes. Yet if we learn to recognize this reaction, we can quiet the voice of shame and use our guilt in a healthy manner to guide us towards things we claim to care about.

In my travels around the world, meeting a diverse range of people that have left the default path, nothing has been more consistent than the reality that most people want to engage with the world and to be useful. Despite many people thinking that their ideal life would be living out the rest of their life on a beach, when given the option of following that path, few people take it.

Author Sebastian Junger, in his book about soldiers who had returned from war, found a similar thing. Despite dealing with post-traumatic stress disorder, many of the soldiers wanted to return to dangerous warzones. Why? Because at war, they felt part of something, deeply connected to the men and women they were serving with. Junger reflected, "humans don't mind hardship, in fact, they thrive on it; what they mind is not feeling necessary."[140] Junger argues that "modern society has perfected the art of making people not feel necessary."

The need to feel useful is a powerful one. This is the hidden upside of the pathless path and a reason why finding work that aligns with what matters to you and makes you feel useful is so important. When you find the conversations you want to take part in and the work you want to keep doing, you start to feel necessary and the whole world opens up.

Remembering What You Forgot

The initial delight is in the surprise of remembering something I didn't know I knew.
    – Robert Frost

As a kid, I spent as much time as I could on the computer. After school, I ran in the door at home and sat down at the computer. I clicked the America Online logo and waited for the phone line to dial a random number somewhere in the United States. Then came the funny noises and I was in! With the World Wide Web in front of me, it was time to play.

I remember the day my father brought home a copy of *DOS for Dummies*. We opened the book at the computer and entered some of the commands. What a thrill! By typing in a few words, I could control the computer. I was hooked. For years afterward, I participated in a wide variety of online activities. I taught myself how to build websites and code in HTML, I joined wrestling role-playing leagues, ran a basketball simulation league, pirated music, traded beanie babies, and sold website templates, and made my first money on the internet.

I followed my curiosity wherever it took me.

As I got older I made a natural transition to working with technology and computers. Oh, wait… that's not what happened. Instead, I followed the default path, seeking out traditional paths to success. This route went through giant companies, where cutting-edge technology and ideas could only be used after a multi-year planning and proposal process. I never saw my interest in technology as something worth following in and of itself; it was always just an advantage for doing great work on my traditional path.

Looking back, I'm a bit embarrassed about ignoring my consistent curiosity towards technology. In high school, I built a weather site where I would predict snow days for my friends, called "Paul Says it Will." In college, where I started to desire a prestigious career, I nevertheless spent my free time making DJ mixes under the name "DJ PoPo Shizzle," ran a blog with friends called S4, and learned how to code. These experiences, which were not part of the default path, clearly foreshadowed my current self-employment in which I coach, consult, build products, and experiment online. Choosing or creating a career working with technology seems obvious now, but due to the forces shaping my desires, I couldn't see it back then.

About two years into my self-employment journey, I realized that most of the activities that excite me involve a computer. When I build websites, launch a podcast, create online courses, use marketing tools, and hang out with friends on Twitter, I am a kid again, sitting in front of that first computer.

My friend Jonny Miller argues that "human existence is an infinitely unfolding process of remembering, forgetting, and remembering again."[141]

To thrive on the pathless path, we must ignore the shiny objects and distractions and strip away the stories that are not our own to remember who we are. One of the biggest concerns people have when they talk to me about quitting their job is how to make money. That is certainly important, but a more interesting path is possible if you start with what brought you alive in the past. Injecting the energy from these pursuits can lead you in a different direction and can help you figure out what to work on while taking the first steps toward creating a life you truly enjoy.

You Are Creative

> Here's the truth you have to wrestle with: the reason that art (writing, engaging, leading, all of it) is valuable is precisely why I can't tell you how to do it. If there were a map, there'd be no art, because art is the act of navigating without a map. Don't you hate that? I love that there's no map. – Seth Godin

You are not creative. At least this is what you tell me. But I don't buy it. I just think you've been duped. We've lost track of our basic human creativity, convincing ourselves that only people who use certain tools or work in advertising or other artistic areas are creative.

Nonsense.

We are all creative. Navigating the bureaucracy of any institution takes a certain kind of creativity. Figuring out which emotion an emoji is expressing requires creativity. Parenting is probably one of the most creative human activities. Learning how to use technology takes creativity. As does hosting a dinner party or organizing a trip with friends, not to mention planning a wedding. If you think planning a modern-day wedding isn't creative, I don't know what to tell you. Detach yourself from conventional notions of what creativity means, and you'll see it everywhere.

Another reason we struggle to see the potential for channeling creativity is that until very recently if you wanted to share your work with the world, you needed permission. You needed access to audiences or distribution channels via gatekeepers, whose sole job was to limit access.

We still haven't fully realized how dramatically this state of affairs has changed. The internet has made it possible for people from anywhere in the world with access to the internet to create and share their ideas, stories, and creations without permission. Seth Godin puts it bluntly: "The world just gave you control over the means of production. Not to master them is a sin."[142]

This book you are reading did not require anyone's permission to be published. I just decided to do it. I wrote it myself, hired editors and designers to help me, and put my name on it as the publisher. You can do this too.

Modes of creative expression that used to require the approval of gatekeepers include publishing books or songs, selling your artwork, starting a radio show, and selling crafts to a mass market, among many others.

If you still want permission, though, **I'm granting it. Go for it.**

Many people struggle to start making a living from their creative endeavors because they are still operating within the logic of the default path. On the default path, you have to get the job before you can do the work. On the pathless path, you simply do the work first and then decide if you want to continue. For example, I wrote online for several years, and after several people asked if I planned to write a book, I decided to raise the stakes and take that next step. It would have been easy to say that I couldn't get published and not bother, but I knew I was capable of writing something worth reading. Just two decades ago, I wouldn't have been able to reach a wide audience. Consider that Stephen King was rejected by 30 publishers before someone agreed to publish his first book. It pains me to think about all the great writers worth reading that gave up before King did.

We tend to think of creativity as a predetermined ability, like someone who might have a genetic advantage to run faster. Instead, I think creativity is more of an active choice and the removal of gatekeepers means that for the first time it might take more energy to deny your own creative expression than exploring it.

A difficulty that remains, however, is figuring out how to get started. This is where people get stuck. A voice in their head asks, "What will people say?"

This is valid. It's scary to share with the world, and if you do it over a long enough period, criticism is inevitable. At first, however, most people run into a different challenge: not having an audience at all. This can be a good thing because it enables you to experiment while building up your confidence slowly.

A deeper fear that's harder to grapple with is the shadow of the gatekeeper system itself, which paired access to an audience with a subtle hostility towards those without the right taste, credentials, or status. While this is fading, you still see examples of this sentiment in popular media. For example, an article published in 2019 in the New York Times titled "Have we hit peak podcasts?" addressed the issue of publication without gatekeepers or restrictions: "...the frequency with which podcasts start...has produced a degree of cultural exhaustion. We're not necessarily sick of listening to interesting programs; but we're definitely tired of hearing from every friend, relative and co-worker who thinks they're just an iPhone recording away from creating the next 'Serial.'"

The message is loud and clear. Podcasts are for serious professionals with the right credentials, and if you don't have them, please don't think of starting one.

We should reject this stance.

While the article makes a valid point about the challenges of making money, it ignores that someone might create something for the sake of it or as a way to learn, connect and feel alive rather than trying to get ahead or get paid.

Creative output is fuel for the pathless path. While my writing hasn't made me famous or rich, it has been vital for staying energized and being able to connect with people that share my curiosities. Growing up, I didn't think I was a creative person. Nor did I think I had permission to share with the world. Luckily, I stopped believing those lies and started to see that there are deeper and more important reasons to create and share. Which brings us to an important question...

Who Do You Serve?

In my first few years of writing online, I let a couple of critical comments get to me. These readers thought that my criticism of the default path was too harsh. Their disapproval stayed in my head and my writing became too safe. But eventually, I realized I wasn't writing for them. I was writing for people like me: those struggling on the default path who want to dream bigger. When I focused on these readers, my writing improved, and I gained a broader audience.

It took me a while to figure out why this was the case but it clicked when I heard a story from Seth Godin about his friend David Chang, who owns the Momofuku Restaurant Group. When Chang opened one of his first restaurants, Godin stopped by and ordered a vegetarian version of a popular dish. Godin returned several times and enjoyed the dish until one day Chang told him, "we only serve it as-is." Godin was sad about not being able to eat the dish but excited for his friend. The reason? Godin knew a secret: once you figure out who you intend to serve, you can go all-in and focus on what it takes to become great.[143]

Thinking we have to serve a mass audience is default path thinking. An industrial, "bigger is better" mindset assumes that everyone is competing in a mass market. In the digital world, it's easy to envision that this mass market is the only competition for the same audiences and attention. However, even if my podcast might sit right next to NPR's *This American Life* in the podcast app, what I am doing is completely different. I am a solo interviewer, editor, graphic designer, and distributor and spend less than $100 per year. NPR has more than 25 people working on that show alone. We have different goals, different audiences, and different reasons for existing.

Figuring out who you want to serve is an important element of the pathless path. On the default path, your job often provides recognition and praise. When you are on your own, without a specific job or colleagues, you may miss that kind of support. This is why it's so important to know what kind of people you want to work with and who you want to serve. Finding the right people, those who might offer support and encouragement along the way can have an outsized effect on your confidence and courage to keep going.

I have benefited from this sort of kindness on my journey, especially early on from my aunt Debbie, Noel, Cam, Jordan, and many others. Tyler Cowen has argued that one of "the most valuable things you can do with your time and with your life" is to believe in people.[144] Being a recipient of this encouragement has inspired me to create a rule for myself: any time I consume something from an individual that inspires me, I have to send them a note to let them know. Creating and sharing in public takes an incredible amount of courage and I remember how awkward and scared I was at the beginning of my journey. It's easy to tell people what they got wrong but much harder to say "I love what you are doing. I hope you keep going and let me know if I can help."

As I've continued to create, share and connect people, I've tapped into a hidden form of motivation, one that is invisible to others. On the default path, promotions, job changes, and raises serve as visible markers of success. However, my proof of success is hidden, coming in the form of messages I receive in my email or conversations with people who are inspired by my work. Lacking a way to "prove" that you are successful can be hard. However, the people that reach out have become my friends, my supporters, and my inspiration, and the reward is far greater than any visible metric of success from my previous path.

These are the people I've decided to serve and it makes my continued journey on the pathless path worth it.

The World Is Waiting

Creativity by nature is an act of boldness and rebellion. – Robert Greene

Maybe I've convinced you that you are creative and that you should ignore the voices that tell you that you should not create. However, you still have some concerns, especially if you are thinking about sharing online. Isn't the internet just filled with scammers or people that want attention?

The fact that those people make you feel uneasy is a good sign. Because the people creating those posts probably don't feel uneasy at all. And this is why I want to urge you to consider sharing with the world. You care. You want to do things in good faith. You want to help people, to listen, and connect with others who share your passions. This doesn't mean you need to build an audience or a business, but what might emerge if you dare to share your writing, painting, dancing, crafts, or other acts of creativity with others? What friends might you meet? What opportunities could you pursue? What communities could you join?

The positive side of earning a living by creating and sharing online or building an online business is often obscured by the logic of the default path, in which the worthiest endeavor is a full-time job. Consider two different people: a mid-level financial analyst at Wells Fargo and someone building a yoga business through Instagram. What's your honest reaction to both people? If you're like I was before I started

157

working on my own, you'd probably be slightly judgmental of the Instagram influencer. Now, I've softened my stance. I've realized the yoga influencer puts their entire reputation at risk and succeeds or fails based on their decisions. As this kind of work becomes more prevalent, our norms will shift and we will question why we are more skeptical of an entrepreneur than the employee at Wells Fargo, a place that has been cited more than 200 times in the last 20 years for fraud, mortgage abuse, and violating investor rights.[145]

Let's recall Ben Hunt's argument that these conventional, full-time paths are no longer industrially necessary, but simply industrially preferable. If we continue to anchor our imagination to default path stories about work, we will continue to ignore the possible paths for our lives.

Even if you do decide that sharing your real work with the world is worthwhile, it's nearly impossible to overcome the sense that you may embarrass yourself. Here it's helpful to remember the "spirit of the fool" and also consider that many people around the world might be waiting for what you have to share.

My public writing journey started on an app called Quora, where I answered users' questions across a wide range of topics. For years I answered the occasional question, mostly on topics I knew a lot about. As I started to enjoy writing more, I created a challenge for myself, answering at least one question at the start of every workday. I expanded the range of topics I wrote about and finally shared a lengthy reflection on my previous health challenges. It was the most vulnerable piece I had ever shared publicly.[146] It had been sitting in a document on my computer for more than two years. I had been scared to share it, convinced that no one would want to read it and that people might make fun of me. But the post reached half a million people and I got countless messages and comments thanking me for sharing:

What an inspirational account. Write a book!!! Thank you so much for sharing, this was truly an enriching read.

It's one of the most amazing and thoughtful answers I've read in a while. Thank you for having the courage of sharing it and I wish you the best.

Just commenting to say that this was an excellent answer/post, and thanks for writing it.

I'm not sick, but I really needed to read this. Wonderful! All the best in your career. I wish I could meet more people in person like you!

Real heroes are ordinary people who had to face extraordinary problems but never gave up and survived. This is you, Paul. Bless you, my friend.

As I read the comments, I realized many people around the world see courage in creation and sharing, and these are the people I now write for.

And this group is diverse. As I've explored a broader range of topics such as self-employment, freelancing, our relationship with work, and building an online business, I've met people from 13 to 75 years old, from the United States to New Zealand to Pakistan to China. As increasing numbers of people all around the world are tapping into the opportunities created by the internet, they are also looking for people like them. There has never been a better and easier time to find and connect with people in a positive way.

So maybe I've convinced you that it's worth sharing, but you don't want to launch a social media brand, start writing online, or publish a book. That's fine too. You can start small or do something in your local community. Host a dinner party in your city or town, start a book club, share a poem or essay you've written with a couple of close friends, or even join a local art class. It doesn't matter how you start but that you start. Once people enter this new, creative mode, they realize that they've been holding back a part of themselves for most of their lives. Deep inside, we all have a desire to engage with the world in creative ways and don't worry, I'm here to cheer you on.

Virtuous Meaning Cycles

Maria Popova, who writes the popular site The Marginalian (formerly Brain Pickings), spends her days reading old books and essays. She's passionate about finding ideas, beauty, and wisdom in these texts and then connecting them in her own unique conversation with the world.

Her reflections on the connection between critical thinking and hope in an interview with Krista Tippett on the On Being podcast helped me transform how I wanted to engage with the world. She argued, "critical thinking without hope is cynicism. But hope without critical thinking is naïveté."[147] I hit rewind and listened to this several times. I knew she was talking to me.

When I first started on my path and began writing, I was driven by frustration. I saw problems with the way we think about work and our lives everywhere, and I wanted everyone to see things like I did. I wanted to be right. My essays and articles were convincing, but they were not inspiring.

It was critical thinking without hope.

This desire for intellectual exploration with others has been a big theme on my journey. But not until I added hope to my critical thinking and embraced a more expansive view of the world did I attract the kind of people I wanted to welcome into my conversation. In my first couple of months in Taiwan, I read a book on writing by William Zinsser. He urged me to "believe in your own identity and your own opinions. Writing is an act of ego, and you might as well admit it. Use its energy to keep yourself going."[148]

In that single moment, I stopped hedging my bets. I would no longer fear what people might think, but I would also leave my cynical edge behind. After reading Zinsser, I put my heart into my writing and made my case. This was the way out of cynicism. I became more optimistic not because I started to write better or was right, but because I stopped hiding. I led with my curiosity, vulnerability, and passion and it immediately attracted the kind of people I wanted to meet.

In the early 1900s, professor and writer Bertrand Russell noted that "any person who visits the Universities of the Western world is liable to be struck by the fact that the intelligent young of the present day are cynical to a far greater extent than was the case formerly."[149]

He argued that developing a cynical stance was necessary in a world in which much of what authorities and leaders claim directly contrasts with what is true. The cure for such cynicism, he said, would "only come when intellectuals can find a career that embodies their creative impulses."[150]

This is possible on the pathless path. You can experiment with your work and your life until you stumble into a virtuous cycle that helps you continue to move in a positive direction. By a virtuous cycle, I mean being able to do work that you enjoy that naturally leads to opportunities and people that help make your life better.

The biggest challenge to creating your virtuous cycle and one of the most dangerous failure modes of the pathless path is cynicism. Many people who leave the default path do so because they've become cynical and are driven by a desire to escape. But escaping is only the first step of leaving a certain path behind. In order to create a sustainable journey and path, it requires finding ways of orienting to the world that leave space for hope.

At the beginning of my journey, I wanted to prove people wrong and that my way of living life was good and right. My writing was cynical because I couldn't express why I cared about those ideas. I was depending more on facts than the songs singing in my soul. When I was brave enough to open my heart, I got more support and that led not only to a better path but a more exciting future.

10

Playing the Long Game

When I quit the New York Times to be a full-time mother, the voices of the world said that I was nuts. When I quit it again to be a full-time novelist, they said I was nuts again. But I am not nuts. I am happy. I am successful on my own terms. Because if your success is not on your own terms, if it looks good to the world but does not feel good in your heart, it is not success at all. – Anna Quindlen

Working Backward

One of the goals of the pathless path is to make commitments: to a type of work, ways of living, creative projects, or a "conversation" with the world. A challenge here, however, is that the possibilities are so vast. Which raises a question: how do you begin to figure out what you want to do when there are not many limits?

On the default path, the kinds of work you can do and the resulting kinds of lives that are possible are limited, helping to simplify this issue.

I never realized how much I was constraining my imagination when I was only considering paths or jobs that already existed. Embracing the pathless path enabled me to see the possibilities for my life. This was exciting but also overwhelming. I often have the sense that I'd need multiple lifetimes to truly test and explore my options.

Instead of embarking on an endless search, I've taken a different approach: working backward. Instead of thinking about what I want to do and how I want to live, I start instead with what I don't want to be doing and what failure looks like. By looking at what might go wrong with our lives, we can avoid obvious traps, creating more space for things to go right.

One useful mental model for thinking about this is the principle of inversion, popularized by German mathematician Carl Jacobi. He told his students to "invert, always invert," encouraging them to approach difficult problems by inverting the equation to gain a new perspective.[151] We can also apply this principle to our lives. For example, instead of asking what makes up an amazing life, we first define the worst-case scenario and then work backward. What does a miserable life entail? What actions would make achieving such a life more likely? Then figure out how you can avoid these things from becoming true.

During my time on the default path, I often imagined a future version of myself that I knew I didn't want to be: an overweight guy in his 50s who barely tolerates the people in his life, hates his job, spends his days in a windowless cubicle farm, and isn't very happy. If you had known me then, you would have said I would never have ended up like that. However, by the time I left my job I was much closer to that person than when I started.

164

On the pathless path, I take this exercise much more seriously. While the grumpy guy in the cubicle is even harder to imagine now, there are still aspects of him that I want to avoid. Here is my current sketch of the person I don't want to be ten years from now:

> *Paul is still committed to the pathless path, a fact that still draws skepticism from other people. He has a couple of kids, but is barely making ends meet and is ashamed of this fact. He goes a few months every year without income and is filled with insecurity about his finances almost all the time. He's too stubborn to take a full-time job and instead of admitting he might be wrong about his approach to life, he angrily tweets about how stupid everyone is working in traditional jobs. This is all complicated by ongoing health issues which limit his energy and sometimes leave him semi-bedridden for weeks at a time.*

The negative future version of me is financially insecure, does not have a predictable income, and is cynical and stubborn. I could become "negative me" by doing the following: spending time with negative and cynical people, not finding supportive friends, not staying open to all kinds of paid work (including full-time employment), obsessing over divisive media and politics, working on things I resent, and not being honest about my own motivations. Inverting helps you identify traps that could derail your efforts to keep your journey alive.

I encourage everyone to write a description of the person you don't want to be, then brainstorm actions that might create that outcome. This exercise may be uncomfortable because undoubtedly you will see traces of the person you imagine in your present life. These traces are clues about what to change in your life right now.

In addition to identifying who we don't want to become, we should seek to identify ways of working and living that might add unnecessary risk to our path. Early in my journey, I identified being a freelancer and having a single type of income as a key risk. This motivated me to try to make money in as many ways as possible, even if it meant sacrificing short-term income to do so.

I was inadvertently embracing a principle that professor Nassim Taleb calls "antifragility." Antifragility is a well-documented natural phenomenon in which things gain strength through disorder. For example, cities are antifragile. While individual businesses in a city may fail in an individual year, the city thrives over the long-term, fueled by new residents, buildings, and businesses.

Like a city with many industries, I want to be resilient to changes in income, shifts in the economy, and rule changes from various platforms that I use. For this reason, in addition to freelancing work, I've built things that allow me to generate income without selling my time and that target different audiences. The first two years after shifting away from freelancing with this approach, my overall income declined substantially. However, a few years later, I now have between eight and ten different ways of making money where I consistently earn at least $200 a month. While the risks of any one of these disappearing is high, the odds that all of them disappear at once is low.

Early on in my journey, I realized that my entire goal was to stay on the pathless path indefinitely. This is what author James Carse calls the "infinite game": "A finite game is played for the purpose of winning, an infinite game for the purpose of continuing the play."[152] By working backward, I realized that the biggest risks for me are spending my time doing things that undermine my ability to stay optimistic and energized, and obviously, running out of money. This is why I've spent so much time focusing on creating the conditions for success and lowering my risk of failure, rather than aiming at success itself.

Almost everyone that stays on the pathless path eventually adopts a similar approach. The reason? The longer you stay on the path, the higher your odds you'll be able to sustain it over the long term. People come to realize that the challenge is not to find work to pay the bills but instead to have time to keep taking chances and exploring opportunities to find the things worth committing to over the long-term.

The Positive Side of Freedom

In the paycheck world, there used to be a saying: dress for the job you want, not the job you have. The analogous idea in the free agent world is: learn to exercise the freedoms you might acquire, not just the freedoms you have. – Venkatesh Rao

Beyond money, the second most common concern people have about working less or building a life less centered around work is what they will do with their time. On the default path, we may not realize how much energy it requires to simply go through the motions and stay on the path, so it's easy to mistake our lack of energy outside of work for a lack of interest in anything else. As a result, we don't know what we'll do when we're no longer "working."

The problem of what to do once you have freedom is something that fascinated writer Erich Fromm. In his book *Escape from Freedom*, he explores how millions across the world struggled to adapt to the newfound freedom they had in their lives in the 1930s.

At this time, people were experiencing greater freedom as the control of religious authorities diminished, workweeks became shorter, and increased prosperity provided new options for living. Many believed that the end of World War I had concluded the struggle for freedom and the only problem left was what to do with it.

Well-educated elites and business owners liberated from the rules of rigid institutions were thrilled, but many others were frustrated. Fromm noticed that many people felt "isolated, powerless, and an instrument of purposes outside of [themselves], alienated from [themselves] and others."[153] To political leaders like Hitler and Stalin, this was great news. They could increase their own power by manipulating the masses with stories that helped them make sense of their lives.

Why would so many people trade some of their newfound freedom to join these authoritarian movements? Fromm argued that the reason lied behind two different types of freedom. First was negative freedom or "freedom from" outside control. Second was positive freedom or the "freedom to" engage with the world in a way that is true to yourself. Fromm's positive version of freedom was much more than the freedom to act. He described it as "the full realization of the individual's potential, together with his ability to live actively and spontaneously." Fromm argued that those freed from oppression but unable to develop a positive version of freedom were destined to be filled with feelings of separateness and anxiety.[154]

People are willing to compromise a lot to suppress these feelings. The stories Nazism offered the masses in the 1930s relieved people of their responsibility to grapple with "freedom to" and make their own decisions. In exchange, the autocratic leaders gave them a script for how to live. Fromm, who was writing at the beginning of World War

II, thought this a terrible mistake, even at the time: "because we have freed ourselves of the older overt forms of authority, we do not see that we have become the prey of a new kind of authority."[155] Abdicating our responsibility to live our own lives can have dire consequences.

Over the last 100 years, the number of ways you can engage with life has exploded beyond imagination. Now, not only political leaders offer narratives for interacting with the world, but also employers, companies, media outlets, and other institutions. Everyone gives you roadmaps for living life and becoming free. You just have to buy their products, embrace their story, or join their company, and instead of having to develop your own agency, the respective institution will make you part of their special group. In his post-World War II writing, Fromm demonstrated that, surprisingly, the urge to conform in this way was most powerful not in Communist societies, but in the West.

The problem with conformity, Fromm argued, is that it leads to an existence that is too rigid, routine, and predictable. This undermines the space for spontaneity and active engagement that might help one discover what matters at a deeper level. David Foster Wallace once argued that this is the whole point of a liberal arts education in perhaps the best defense of this tradition:

> *I submit that this is what the real, no-bullshit value of your liberal arts education is supposed to be about: how to keep from going through your comfortable, prosperous, respectable adult life dead, unconscious, a slave to your head and to your natural default setting of being uniquely, completely, imperially alone day in and day out.*[156]

Wallace's point is that doing what almost everyone else is doing is the natural thing in life. If we are serious about other approaches, it will take work.

In his own writing, Fromm continued to explore the topic of freedom for several decades after World War II. In his book *The Art of Loving,* he argued that the root of a positive version of freedom is a deep sense of connectedness with the world. A path to achieve this state was through "creative activity." He offered examples: "whether a carpenter makes a table, or a goldsmith a piece of jewelry, whether the peasant grows his corn or the painter paints a picture, in all types of creative work the worker and his object become one, man unites himself with the world in the process of creation." As he said, in a world where we are pushed to "regard our personal qualities and the result of our efforts as commodities that can be sold for money, prestige, and power," engaging in a creative endeavor allows us to find value in the act itself.[157]

I've already made a case for you to find a way to create, either publicly or privately. However, Fromm presents another deeper reason. In addition to doing something challenging, "finding the others," or discovering a different kind of work you enjoy, you might also find a mode of being that opens you up to a deeper relationship with the world and yourself. In this way, the creative act is one of the most sacred things in the world and should be taken seriously in itself and not with any expected outcome.

Before I left my job, I was exploring my creativity but did not feel the deeper connectedness that Fromm wrote about. I was convinced that escaping my job was the most important thing I had to do. However, soon after achieving the "freedom from" traditional employment, I discovered the vastness and challenge of developing a positive side of freedom.

Ultimately, figuring out what to do with freedom once we have it is one of the biggest challenges of the pathless path. Writer Simon Sarris argues that we can only do this by increasing our capacity for agency, or our ability to take deliberate action in the world. He argues, "the secret of the world is that it is a very malleable place, we must be sure that people learn this, and never forget the order: Learning is naturally the consequence of doing."[158] In other words, only by taking action do we learn and only by learning do we discover what we want. Without this, we will struggle to take advantage of the freedom that the pathless path offers. We are ultimately the ones that determine our fate, and without expressing agency, we struggle to be free.

In the arc of history, the freedom to explore the possibilities of our lives is a relatively recent phenomenon. For the amount of attention that the idea of freedom receives, there is still relatively little expression of it at the individual level. The default path has given us the freedom to earn money and spend it as we please, work in different fields, and have some control over our lives, but keeps many trapped in a pseudo-freedom where one is free from absolute oppression but not free enough to act with a high degree of agency.

The pathless path is the deliberate pursuit of a positive version of freedom. Revisiting Fromm's definition, "the full realization of the individual's potential, together with his ability to live actively and spontaneously," we see that developing our own sense of agency is vital.[159] Thus, figuring out what to do with your time is a real concern.

For this, I've found no better advice than the following from Dolly Parton: "Find out who you are and do it on purpose."[160]

Reinventing Who You Are

Imagine it's 1980. You are 22 years old, freshly graduated from college. You take a job at General Motors, one of the biggest companies in the world. On your first day, you walk into your office and see a flat metal desk with an electronic typewriter, a rotary phone, and a physical inbox with two slots, one for incoming memos and the other for outgoing.

You spend the next 20 years at General Motors and receive several promotions. When computers are introduced, you volunteer to be an early adopter and do your best to stay up to date with the latest technology. Despite this, you get laid off in the 2001 recession and spend the next ten years jumping between different automotive parts suppliers. In 2010, you join a startup that builds driverless cars because they're looking for someone with industry connections. You feel like you're operating at the edge of your competence, but you manage to get by. In 2015, your career comes full circle when you re-join General Motors to help your old manager with a new product line.

In 2020, your entire team starts working remotely. You learn how to use Zoom and Slack, and you seem to know what you're doing on both your computer and mobile phone. You are shocked at how quickly the younger team members adapt to this new normal. You can keep up, but you find it all exhausting. You sense it might be time to hang it up and decide that at the end of 2020, you will retire.

Here's a question for you: do you think the next forty years will see more or less change?

When we think about the future, we tend to underestimate how much things will change, especially for ourselves. Researchers call this the

172

"end of history illusion." Across all age groups, people indicate that they have experienced profound change in the past but when they forecast their future, they don't see the trend continuing. People believe that "the pace of personal change has slowed to a crawl and that they have recently become the people they will remain."[161]

What can we do with this knowledge? For me, it's made me more enthusiastic about embracing the pathless path because if I'm going to change more than I can expect, I might as well attempt to shape those changes. This is an alternative to how many people deal with change: by denying, delaying, or rejecting it. As we age we do become more mentally rigid and minor challenges to our routines can be landmines threatening to blow up our weeks, and suggestions that we live in new ways are treated as acts of war.

Moving abroad, running my own business, and living in more than 20 places in only a few years have made me much more resilient to change and more aware of my own default to become rigid in my thinking. I've become more capable of proactively embracing change, but I'd be lying if I said I am excited about every new shift in my environment, schedule, and work. Nonetheless, I've come to see reinvention as one of the most valuable meta-skills worth developing, and on the other side of these experiments, I am often much more relaxed and confident than before.

Professor and author Yuval Harari argued that "in order to keep up with the world of 2050, you will need not merely to invent new ideas and products, but above all to reinvent yourself again and again."[162] Nothing has helped me improve this skill more than living in other countries. People often ask me how to prepare for living abroad. My response? You can't, and when you leave the place you know, you will inevitably face challenges. From forgetting my passport on the other side of Italy to a stray dog biting me in Taiwan and a parasite infection in Mexico, I've dealt with scary uncertainty head-on. I wouldn't encourage you to seek out these experiences, but it does raise a question: if coping with these challenges increased my confidence, is comfort overrated?

As more people invent new paths and enter new environments, communities, and online worlds, many will be forced out of their comfort zone. The sooner this happens the better because the era of living your entire life in a small, local, and familiar community is over.

Whether we want to or not, we'll have to keep reinventing ourselves.

Embracing Abundance

My cousin has a saying that has always stuck with me: "it will even out when we are dead." More than fatalism, this is an invitation to a relationship built on generosity, one that's deeper than keeping a balance of accounts. Developing such a spirit of generosity and a mindset of abundance is increasingly a challenge in today's world, where much of what we do is filtered by how much things cost and how we "spend" our time.

This way of seeing the world is the result of a slow but steady transformation of how we relate to both time and the economy. Until the 1600s when clocks became ubiquitous, people rarely thought about time. English historian E.P. Thompson noted that instead, people thought in terms of activities. In Madagascar, a half-hour was a "rice cooking," and a brief moment was "frying a locust." When they had clocks, people increasingly thought about time as something related to money. Thompson noted that "time is now currency, it is not passed but spent."[163]

Today we think about how we "spend" time, if we are getting "our money's worth," if we are getting or giving value, and the "cost" of our actions. By equating time with money, we can make trade-offs, calculations, and coordinate global meetings, but we also decrease any sense of abundance. This shift has coincided with incredible advancements in our economy and its ability to deploy almost anything we want across the world, but at the same time has undermined our own security. In the 1970s, academic turned farmer Wendell Berry wrote about how economic success includes the hidden cost of depriving people "of any independent access to the staples of life: clothing, shelter, food, even water."[164] What was once the riches of self-reliance have become things with a price.

Figuring out how to escape these patterns of thinking is vital to keeping the pathless path journey alive. I've done this over the past few years by looking at generosity as not merely a trait, but a skill that needs to be practiced. Practicing this skill has opened me up to a hidden side of life, filled not only with abundance, but also meaningful connection.

I realized that this skill is worth practicing when I read a book called *Sacred Economics* by Charles Eisenstein. In it, he introduces the idea of a gift economy which he argues has been with humans for ages. He compares it to our default economic mindset:

> *Whereas money today embodies the principle, "More for me is less for you," in a gift economy, more for you is also more for me because those who have, give to those who need it. Gifts cement the mystical realization of participation in something greater*

than oneself which, yet, is not separate from oneself. The axioms of rational self-interest change because the self has expanded to include something of the other.[165]

Most of us have experienced this type of gift-giving in our families. As children, very little is asked of us in the economic realm. Even as we grow into adulthood, it would be odd for our parents to keep meticulous track of what we owe them. Similarly, among close friends, there is often an unspoken acknowledgment that aiming for absolute fairness is never the goal. Like my cousin, for whom "it will even out when we are dead," we see the wisdom in supporting deeper relationships.

However, operating in the spirit of a gift economy outside of our close connections is uncomfortable and it's probably not something we should embrace in the broadest sense. If we had to form deep, meaningful relationships with everyone we interacted with within the economy, it would grind to a halt. However, the opposite is also true. When we look to the market to solve all our needs, it leaves us feeling empty. Professor Tim Wu made this point in a widely read essay titled "The Tyranny of Convenience," where he argues that convenience, "with its promise of smooth, effortless efficiency…threatens to erase the sort of struggles and challenges that help give meaning to life."[166]

Wu argues that many see convenience as a form of liberation. People aim for "financial independence" only to realize when they achieve it that they're only independent in the narrow sense of being able to pay for everything. Realizing the flaws in this kind of economic thinking and inspired by writers like Eisenstein and Berry, I decided to experiment with the gift economy in my work. Based on Eisenstein's book, I embraced three guiding principles:

1. Find ways to give without expectation of anything in return.
2. Be willing to receive gifts in any form and on any timeline.
3. Be open to being wrong about all of this and adjust my approach as necessary.

With this in mind, I looked for places to give what I had to offer. My first practical experiment with the gift economy involved a spontaneous decision at the end of a coffee conversation with a stranger I met through the Couchsurfing app in Boston. She shared that she was running out of money and had been making a living working on various projects and relying on the kindness of strangers as she traveled around the United States. As we were about to part ways, I asked her, "Would you be comfortable receiving a cash gift from me?" A bit shocked, she said yes. I sent her $100 via a payment app and walked away.

When the thought first popped into my head, I noticed inner voices that told me it was a bad idea: "What if she wastes the money?" "Won't this make her too lazy to take a job that might help her?" "She doesn't deserve it." Until that moment, I had always listened to those voices and leaned away from discomfort. However, this is the whole point of embracing the gift mindset and practicing generosity. It exposes our default scripts about how we think the world should work and opens us up to new possibilities.

A couple weeks later I received an unprompted message. She told me that she had used the money to become a member on HomeAway, a site where hosts offer free lodging and food in exchange for work, typically no more than 4-5 hours per day, in places like farms, restaurants, and hotels. She had found a place that would host her for a couple of months and she was pretty excited about it.

Partly because in today's world most people donate to formal charities, giving directly feels weird. Many charitable organizations are set up like businesses and use the same marketing tactics. Giving $100 to a charity online feels normal and comfortable. Handing over a $100 bill to a stranger feels reckless. "What if they_____?" Fill in the blank with your preferred worry. While I've never fully overcome these voices, giving to strangers over and over again has shown me that our default assumptions often stop us from doing things that are not only good and meaningful but might even make our lives better.

Eisenstein argues that in a gift economy, "gifts flow toward the greatest need," and in learning to deal with the discomfort of a gifting mindset, I've been able to more clearly see those who might need some help while also being on the receiving end of unexpected offers of generosity from people from around the world.

I've also embraced the spirit of a gift economy in my work. I run an online course that's priced for knowledge workers based in the Western economy. For many of the people taking the course, the price is much less than a day's salary. Yet for people in other countries, it can be more than a month's salary. From the beginning, I integrated a gift economy approach into my course. In my first iteration, I included an option to "click here if you can't afford this and I'll send you a free version of the course." As you might expect, no one purchased the course and requests flowed in steadily. Unfortunately, no one ever opened the course either.

To design a better approach, I applied what I had learned in my interactions with philosopher Andrew Taggart.[167] I introduced language saying that I wanted anyone motivated to learn to be able to access the course. I created an online exercise that shared my own goals ("to support my life doing this kind of teaching and creative work") and included questions about their motivation and their plan for finishing the course as well as space to share their financial challenges if they wished. At the end of the exercise, I asked them three questions:

1. What is the low range of a price you would be willing to offer for an online course?
2. What is the high range of a price you would be willing to offer for an online course?
3. What is a gift that "feels right" for this course that you are able to give wholeheartedly?

In contrast to my free offer, which ended up being a quick transaction that didn't help anyone, this version enabled people to get to know me on a deeper level and share a bit about themselves. It was an invitation to a deeper relationship. In the past few years, I've received nearly 500 submissions and the applications never cease to amaze me.

One person from Vietnam said that the course costs more than their monthly salary. Impressed with my generosity, however, this person detailed a plan to repay me over the coming years. The response explained how the course would further the person's career and increase their salary. In such cases, I try to give them the course for free or in exchange for small gifts. Yet the amount of generosity that exists in the world always blows me away. All you have to do is open yourself up to this mode of being.

Seth Godin reminds us that the internet has "lowered the marginal cost of generosity" and I'm not sure most people realize the potential of this development. In the near future, people will have public digital wallets, and transmitting cash to someone we know or just met will be an ordinary event. This is why thinking about generosity as a skill and looking for opportunities to practice is important.

To understand the power of a gift, you must first open yourself up to receive. This is easier said than done. Opening yourself to generosity often means grappling with your own insecurities about not feeling responsible. When I first started writing publicly, I created a Patreon, which allows people to make micro-donations to support someone's work. I announced this in the context of my plan to embrace the gift economy. Within hours of sending this first email, two friends, Jordan and Noel, immediately supported me for $3 a month. Their support wasn't going to secure my future, but the effects were profound. A feeling of gratitude filled my heart. Their small vote of confidence increased mine as well. I also felt like I needed to pay them back, not monetarily but with my courage to keep going on my path.

Eisenstein also realized the significance of relationships within the gift economy:

> One thing that gifts do is that they create ties among people — which is different from a financial transaction. If I buy something from you, I give you the money and you give me the thing, and we have no more relationship after that. I don't owe you anything, you don't owe me anything. The transaction is finished. But if you give me something, that's different because now I kind of feel like I owe you one. It could be a feeling of obligation, or you could say it's a feeling of gratitude. [168]

The benefits of embracing the spirit of a gift economy are invisible to the people who ask me how I plan to monetize, scale, and grow my business. I'm not in the business of being a business. I'm embracing the work of building a life and all of the connections that will make that meaningful.

When you find the work you want to keep doing, what makes it meaningful is that you are drawn to do it for its own sake. Seth Godin says that each of us carries an artist inside for whom it is imperative that we find the work we want to keep doing. Godin claims that this work is about more than getting paid: "You cannot create a piece of art merely for money. Doing it as part of commerce so denudes art of wonder that it ceases to be art."[169]

Beyond appreciating the work you want to do, embracing the spirit of a gift economy is a way to transcend our modern default assumptions about our value in the world to allow wonder, creativity, and connection to emerge and plant seeds inside us and the people around us. Through experiments over the past five years, I've realized that not only is generosity a skill worth practicing, but it has compounding benefits over time.

I agree with what Eisenstein noted in his study of gift economies "it's the generous person who is the wealthiest."[170] The world may not fully agree, but at least in my little corner of the world, I can pretend it's true and have a little more fun.

Coming Alive Over Getting Ahead

*The true scholar grudges every opportunity of action passed by,
as a loss of power.*
– Ralph Waldo Emerson

Everyone on the pathless path eventually needs to develop a strategy for approaching their journey. On the pathless path, once you open yourself up to possibilities and start experimenting with different ways of working and living, the biggest problem is the paradox of choice. There are too many interesting things worth doing and too many places to visit. To prioritize, developing a set of principles to help you make decisions is essential.

My personal principles are sprinkled throughout this book. These ideas, principles, questions, and mental models for how I think about everything from money to relationships to work are always evolving and shifting.

One of my most important is the mantra "coming alive over getting ahead." I embraced this fundamental shift when I left my previous path, and the mantra reminds me that I don't want to create another job for myself.

When I see an opportunity to make money, scale something, charge more money, or move faster, this phrase reminds me to explore all possibilities first, including doing nothing.

In April of 2020, the online consulting skills course I created 18 months earlier started making more money, driven by the widespread adoption of remote work during the Covid-19 pandemic. I had been tinkering with the course for a couple of years at that point but never expected it to be anything more than a minor side project. Yet for almost all of 2020, the course generated an average of $5,000 per month, giving me a clear signal that it was more sustainable than I thought.

As someone with more than ten years of experience in the business world, every bone in my body was telling me to think about how to grow it further. At the end of the year, I was invited to join an intensive course and coaching group for people generating consistent income through online courses. The leaders felt that I had an opportunity to make a lot more money by taking a different approach with my course. I agreed with their assessment, but something was holding me back.

Before committing, I spent a couple of days reflecting on the decision, asking myself, "What would I end up doing with the increased earnings?" I decided I would use the time to write. Then I realized that there was nothing stopping me from doing that at that moment. So I decided that instead of scaling my course, I would write this book.

Coming alive over getting ahead.

After my initial frenzied efforts to land freelance projects, I reflexively said "no" to many paths to making more money. This meant more financial insecurity, but I was doing it because I didn't want to fall into the trap of creating another "job" for myself. This ultimately paid off as the space I created enabled me to be creative, become more resilient, and find a positive way to engage with my work and the world.

At many steps along the journey, when I see an opportunity to make more money or pursue something that would require me to scale beyond a "company of one," I pause. I spent ten years on a path where making numbers go up was always the way forward. Now I'm on a path where that is one option of many, and as I've experienced the beauty and aliveness of opening myself up to different modes of life such as creating, non-doing, and connecting with others, I now understand clearly the value of doing things outside of work.

This is one thing I think people get wrong about keeping options open.

On the default path, optionality can be a trap. This is because you are trapped within your own career narrative. On the pathless path, however, optionality can pay consistent dividends because you are not holding out for another job but leaving space for a little more life.

Create Your Own Culture

Why am I doing all this? Why does it matter so much?

I have bold aspirations. They may not be legible, measurable, or understandable to you, but they give my life a direction and a purpose.

In sum, the goal of being on this path is:

Being able to get to a state of being where I can spend almost all my time helping, supporting, and inspiring others to do great things with their lives.

This is why *Tuesdays with Morrie* makes me cry every time I read it. Because I think Professor Morrie Schwartz pulled it off.

When writer Mitch Albom saw his old professor on TV, he was shocked to see someone who had left a strong impression on him many years earlier but had drifted out of his life.

Morrie was on NBC's program *Nightline* sharing the lessons he had learned since being diagnosed with Lou Gehrig's disease, associated with a steady decline and eventual death. Albom wondered how sixteen years had passed since they had last seen each other. He knew he had to see Morrie as soon as possible.

During those sixteen years, Albom had become a successful sportswriter and entertainer. He had a column at the Detroit Free Press, had written multiple books, and even made appearances on radio and television shows. Work was his life:

> *I stopped renting. I started buying. I bought a house on a hill. I bought cars. I invested in stocks and built a portfolio. I was cranked to a fifth gear, and everything I did, I did on a deadline. I exercised like a demon. I drove my car at breakneck speed. I made more money than I had ever figured to see. I met a dark-haired woman named Janine who somehow loved me despite my schedule and the constant absences. We married after a seven-year courtship. I was back to work a week after the wedding. I told her – and myself – that we would one day start a family, something she wanted very much. But that day never came.*
>
> *Instead, I buried myself in accomplishments, because with accomplishments, I believed I could control things, I could squeeze in every last piece of happiness before I got sick and died, like my uncle before me, which I figured was my natural fate.*[171]

Albom was succeeding on the default path. Yet seeing Morrie on the screen ignited a personal crisis. He reflected on his dreams of becoming a musician, joining the Peace Corps, and living in beautiful places: "I traded lots of dreams for a bigger paycheck, and I never even realized I was doing it."[172]

Drawn perhaps by his own yearning to ask deeper questions about his life, or by a hunch that there was something more to find, or that his own emerging conversation with the world might lead to wisdom, he headed to Cambridge, Massachusetts, to talk with Morrie.

Albom planned one visit, but Morrie insisted he come back. Their conversations, held over a period of several weeks, would turn into a book called *Tuesdays with Morrie*, with millions of copies sold worldwide. The book is powerful not only because of Morrie's passion for life, but also Albom's own transformation. He and Morrie discussed the same challenges and questions that I dealt with over the past several years that I've explored in this book.

In one significant quote, Morrie reflects on the difference between living and dying:

> *"Dying," Morrie suddenly said, "is only one thing to be sad over, Mitch. Living unhappily is something else. So many of the people who come to visit me are unhappy." Why? "Well, for one thing, the culture we have does not make people feel good about themselves. We're teaching the wrong things. And you have to be strong enough to say if the culture doesn't work, don't buy it. Create your own."*[173]

If the culture doesn't work, don't buy it. Create your own.

This is what the pathless path is all about. It's having the courage to walk away from an identity that seems to make sense in the context of the default path in order to aspire towards things you don't understand. It's to experiment in new ways, to remix your own path, to develop your own personal definition of freedom, and to dare to have faith that it will be okay, no matter how much skepticism, insecurity, or fear you face.

Morrie pulled it off too. He created his own culture. A Brandeis professor on the surface with the spirit of the pathless path underneath. Here is how Albom described Morrie's world:

> *Morrie, true to these words, had developed his own culture – long before he got sick. Discussion groups, walks with friends, dancing to his music in the Harvard Square church. He started a project called Greenhouse, where poor people could receive mental health services. He read books to find new ideas for his classes, visited with colleagues, kept up with old students, wrote letters to distant friends. He took more time eating and looking at nature and wasted no time in front of TV sitcoms or "Movies of the Week." He had created a cocoon of human activities – conversation, interaction, affection – and it filled his life like an overflowing soup bowl.*[174]

Morrie lived life to its fullest. He didn't have any regrets when he lost the ability to sing, dance, swim, and walk. He told Albom, "I may be dying, but I am surrounded by loving, caring souls. How many people can say that?"[175] These conversations affected Albom profoundly, convincing him to change his mindset completely:

> *And you know, you can either choose to just see the world as all gloom, but I think I learned from Morrie early on that, you know, he was dying from Lou Gehrig's disease and...he couldn't move, he couldn't – he had to be lifted out of a chair. He had to have someone wipe his rear end. And he was eminently upbeat and positive and still looking to his dying day to the – to the positivity of people and the goodness of people. And I thought if he could do that in a chair where he can't move...then certainly with health and so many blessings, I can certainly be optimistic and try to be*

inspiring to people, too.[176]

After Morrie passed, Albom created more space in his life for activities not centered around work and dedicated himself to broadening the circle of people he sought to help. He started multiple charities to support disadvantaged children, volunteered with organizations that assist the homeless, and helped start an orphanage in Haiti. While he never had kids himself, in 2013 Albom adopted one of the residents of the orphanage in Haiti after she was diagnosed with brain cancer. She came to live with him and his wife in the United States. Although she lost her life, this pushed Albom to continue sharing the wisdom of the people who have come into his life and to be an inspiration to others.

He was following Morrie's advice: Create your own culture.

Those words have stuck with me. When I was working as a consultant, I researched organizational culture. While often misunderstood in the business world, the concept of culture is pretty straightforward. It consists of an evolving set of assumptions that people use to make decisions. And the result of those actions is what shapes the culture.

To create your own culture on the pathless path you must identify the assumptions you make in your approach to life. Here are some of my assumptions, many of which have been sprinkled throughout this book:

- Many people are capable of more than they believe.
- Creativity is a real path to optimism, meaning, and connection.
- We don't need permission to engage with the world and people around us.
- We are all creative, and it takes some people longer to figure that

out.

- Leisure, or active contemplation, is one of the most important things in life,
- There are many ways to make money, and when an obvious path emerges, there is often a more interesting path not showing itself.
- Finding the work that matters to us is the real work of our lives.

Could I be wrong about these things? Definitely. But the pathless path is not about being right. It's about finding ideas and principles worth committing to and seeing where you end up. Without doing this, you are accepting the logic of the default path.

Unfortunately, embracing the pathless path means accepting that you might not know what you are doing and you might look like a fool. This is exactly how I felt in those first few months. But luckily many people have gone before me. I was guided by people like Morrie and Mitch Albom, and others, like Rebecca Solnit, who showed me that getting lost was simply the understanding that "the world has become larger than your knowledge of it."[177]

The pathless path is about opening yourself up to this emergence. It's about growing up and letting go. It's about realizing that if I claim to care about something, I need to be willing to act, and also be willing to be wrong. I must let go of my ego and my need to be seen as a "successful" person. I still feel lost in the sense that I don't know what form my path will take in the future and what publishing this book means for my life. Those thoughts are scary and exciting.

I wouldn't have it any other way.

My life won't look exactly like Morrie's, but I hope that I can channel the spirit of his wisdom. It's rare to find someone at the end of their life that is still so energized and excited about life. I hope I can make it there in that state too.

But the real question is this – are you coming with me?

Go Find Out

I didn't write this book to provide you with a set of how-to instructions for embracing the pathless path. Instead, I want to inspire you to dream a little bit bigger, add some nuance to how you think about life decisions, and give you models and ideas that might enable you to embrace the spirit of the pathless path.

After reading this book, you should no longer be able to look at your current path and think, "this is definitely the only way." Instead, I hope you are able to shift to a place where you know that you have more freedom than you think, and your path can become something you choose again every day.

We are living in a time when it's possible for more and more people to design a life in which they can thrive. Yet many look at that possibility and say, "no thanks," because it means discomfort, uncertainty, and a higher risk of failure. I shared my story because I want to show you that even though you may experience all of those things on the pathless path, the journey can still be worth it.

And it might be the only sensible option left.

We invent the stories we use to guide our lives, and these stories will continue to evolve. Due to many factors, many of our current cultural scripts and stories have calcified over several generations and have stopped working as reliably as they have in the past. This has left large numbers of people around the world confused and frustrated with their relationship to work.

In the first year of leaving my job, everything I thought I knew about the world crumbled as though it had always been an obvious illusion. This was hard to deal with, but I had a lot of support from my friends Stephen Warley and Nita Baum, who had been on their own pathless paths for many years. I often asked them, "Is everyone blind to this, or am I the crazy one?" The answer, I realized, was a bit of both. You must be a little crazy to go against the grain of what most people think. Yet we should remind ourselves that these "experiments in living" as John Stuart Mill called them, are vital to pushing culture forward.

During the Covid-19 pandemic, many people around the world were forced to work remotely. Suddenly what I had been writing about for years became poignant for many people. Sitting at home, knocked out of their daily rhythms, people confessed to me that they were shocked at how much of their identity was wrapped up in work and how lost they had become in their own lives. They wanted to find a new way forward.

This book is my proposal for a new way forward.

Which means things are in your hands now. To help you on your journey, I've put together a list of ten things. This is both a summary of many of the lessons from this book as well as a challenge for you as you embrace the spirit of the pathless path.

First, **question the default**. For many years, I stuck with a story about how I thought my life should go. I assumed there was only one option for structuring my life, around full-time work. I tried to be a "good egg" but ultimately, found myself unhappy with the direction my life was headed. I stumbled into a pathless path and slowly realized that a rigid version of the default path that existed in my mind was only one option of many.

Second, **reflect**. When I started reflecting on my true self, I was able to start building a life around the things I valued. Most of us run on autopilot through life but we can break out of this mode by considering even the simplest reflection exercises. For me creating a daily reminder of four priorities that mattered to me and revisiting the leadership principles I aspired to in grad school helped me see that the gap between what I claimed to care about and how I was living was larger than I wanted. Through reflection, I was able to see that there was a larger "conversation" I was meant to have with the world.

Third, **figure out what you have to offer**. In our desire to be successful, we forget to notice how we are having an impact on others. One of the easiest ways to begin this exploration is to send a message to a few close friends, asking them, "when have you seen me at my best self?" Their responses may surprise you and, perhaps, delight you. We all have stories about who we think we are and why we must be that way but often, others have a better perspective on what makes us stand out.

Fourth, **pause and disconnect**. To improve your relationship with work, I believe it is necessary to disconnect. Unfortunately, a typical one or two-week vacation isn't going to cut it. I believe that the minimum effective dose is at least a month away from work. While this may seem impossible or terrifying, this intervention has a near-universal approval rating and can have a profound effect on your confidence about the future. If a month is scary, I suggest blocking off a random Tuesday afternoon, or another day in the workweek. Don't tell anyone what you are doing and go wander. Go for a long walk, a bike ride, or sit by a river. Pay attention to the feelings that come up and see what they are telling you.

Fifth, **go make a friend**. Venture out of your existing bubble and reach out to someone who has taken an interesting path. Ask them how they got started, what motivates them, and how they think about navigating their life. Most people are much more enthusiastic about sharing what they've learned in their lives than we expect. To embrace the pathless path, you need friends and all you need at the start is one person. Over time, designing your work in a way that will help you naturally "find the others," can be one of the most rewarding things of being on the pathless path and one of the most valuable things you can do in life.

Sixth, **go make something**. Remember, you are creative! Almost everyone has a desire to create something and to put their energy into the world in a positive way. It's just that the legacy of the default path has convinced people that they need permission. But you know this is not true anymore. Find a way to create. Host a dinner party, organize a volunteer event, write a blog post, start journaling in the morning, paint a picture, or host a cooking class for your friends. It doesn't matter what you do, but the sooner you figure out a way to create and share with the world, the faster you'll be able to move closer to finding the activities you want to continue doing throughout your life.

Seventh, **give generously**. Generosity is not only an amount of money, it is a skill we need to practice. It is a way of orienting towards the world that will help you start to understand your own definition of "enough," grapple with your hidden money scripts, and enable you to decouple your belief that security and money are perfectly linked. You don't need to embrace the gift economy completely. Instead, you just need to pay attention and start making offers to share or give when the opportunity emerges. If you don't have an idea, I'll give you an easy way out: you can gift this book to someone that might enjoy it. Ultimately giving is a superpower on the pathless path and will enable you to transcend feelings of separateness and connect more deeply to the people around you.

Eighth, **experiment**. The default path does not leave much space for experimenting with different ways of structuring your life. On the pathless path, you can prototype a change, work in different ways, take extended breaks, live in different countries, test your money beliefs, embrace unique fixed-point goals, and create things you never thought were possible. Remember, the goal is not to get rich but always to figure out what to do next.

Ninth, **commit**. Many people falsely think that escaping work is something worth aiming towards. I thought this at first but realized I had only thought about work as the things you do within a job. What I really wanted was the opportunity to feel useful and to do things that challenged me to grow. This is why I believe that the "real work of your life" is searching for the things you want to commit to and that make your life meaningful. Once you find them, you can dedicate your time to creating the environment to make those things happen.

Finally, **be patient**. In a famous letter to his friend Hume, Hunter S. Thompson argued that searching for the right path in life was important, even if it required many attempts. He told Hume that if he tried eight different paths and failed, that he must keep searching:

"you must find a ninth path."[178] Embracing the pathless path can be a slow and frustrating journey, one that happens at a different speed for everyone. It took me years to build up the courage to quit my job and then several more years to find a mix of work, people, and a way of orienting in the world that felt like it was a path I was meant to be on. Don't rush things. Remember: nothing good gets away, as long as you create the space to let it emerge.

The only thing left to do? Go and see what might happen if you dare to seek out, as the Poet Mary Oliver has called your "one wild and precious life."[179]

I hope you do because I'm always looking for more friends to join me along the way.

Acknowledgements

Writing this book has been a good opportunity to reflect on my life. One of the things that is clear out is how lucky I've been. I've been surrounded by so many good influences that it seems a bit unfair.

I owe the biggest thanks to my parents, Nancy and Bob, for giving me a childhood where I was loved and encouraged. This enabled me to become a confident adult, find success on the default path, and eventually have the courage to carve my own. In addition, I need to thank almost everyone in my extended family. I grew up surrounded by loving siblings, aunts, uncles, grandparents, and cousins, on both sides of my family, all of which have made silent appearances in this book through their inspiration on my life.

Next, I want to thank my wife, Angie. She's been my biggest supporter since we've met. While she's not literally in every chapter of this book, her spirit flows throughout the entire thing. When I told her about the "pathless path" idea from David Whyte's book early on in our relationship she loved it too. When we got married she created a journal for us with the words "The Pathless Path" on the cover as something we could use to reflect on our travels and life. She hates taking credit for anything but meeting her was a big impetus for me being able to shift away from a state of scarcity, wanting to escape life and work, and towards one where I wanted to commit more deeply to building an online business, writing, and owning my own unique path (with her, of course).

I've been lucky to have had many great mentors in school and at work. In college, Dr. Lease-Butts was one of the first, challenging me to do things that were hard. Even though I took her classes as part of my "hoop-jumping" attempts to get "easy A's," I probably learned more about my potential in those classes than any others. In consulting, I was lucky to have several great managers. Christine, Omeed, Peter, and Yvonne were managers that treated me as a person first, worker second, while still pushing me to grow.

After quitting my job, I somehow attracted a small group of enthusiastic supporters. Aunt Debbie, Noel, Cam, Jordan, and Jeremy all had an absurd level of belief in my ability to figure things out and always encouraged me to "keep going." Nita, Stephen, and Jonny were my greatest friends and co-conspirators who were deeply on their own pathless paths. I'm grateful for their wisdom, friendship, and companionship. I'm also especially thankful that Jonny handed me that David Whyte book in the summer of 2018. It changed my life and led to this book.

Along the way, I've been inspired by many people on their own pathless paths, and have learned many things from fellow pathless path participants like Andrew, Michael, Kyle, Tom, Robbie, Jacqueline, Venkatesh, Lydia, Khe, Oshan, Jay, Erv, Matthew, Darren, Travis, Howard, Nemo, Janet, Damien, and Kris not to mention many others. I also want to thank Amy McMillen for writing about her own experiences after leaving her job in *Reclaiming Control*. The existence of her book convinced me that I needed to share my own journey too.

When I started this book, I thought I was a decent writer. Thirteen months later, I now sense I'm still just getting started. John Adamus, Ranjit Saimbi, Paula Trucks-Pape, and Sasha Chapin all helped improve my writing in substantially different but equally powerful ways. In addition, I'd love to thank Thomas Hollands, Valerie Zhang, Oshan Jarow, Stephen Laskowski, Maria Mercedes Otero, and Antoine Buteau for reading various drafts of my book and encouraging me to keep going every step of the way. Finally, thank you to Jon, Lauren, Zakk, and Sadie for offering great vibes and hospitality during the final intensive week of editing at Creator Cabins.

Notes

INTRODUCTION

1   Whyte, David. The Three Marriages: Reimagining Work, Self and Relationship. Reprint, Riverhead Books, 2010.

2   Berntsen, D., and Rubin, D. C. (2004). Cultural life scripts structure recall from autobiographical memory. Memory & Cognition, 32(3), 427–442. doi:10.3758/bf03195836

3   Janssen, S. M. J., & Haque, S. (2017). The transmission and stability of cultural life scripts: a cross-cultural study. Memory, 26(1), 131–143. doi:10.1080/09658211.2017.1335327

4   Keynes, John Maynard. The General Theory of Employment, Interest, and Money. First, Harcourt, Brace & World, 2016.

5   OECD. "Employment: Expected Number of Years in Retirement, by Sex." OECD, 2018, stats.oecd.org/index.aspx?queryid=54758

6   Rosten, Leo. "The Myths by Which We Live." The Rotarian, Sept. 1965, p. 55.

GETTING AHEAD

7   Deresiewicz, William. "The Disadvantages of an Elite Education." The American Scholar, 1 Nov. 2017, theamericanscholar.org/the-disadvantages-of-an-elite-education.

8   "Survey Finds Grade Inflation Continues to Rise at Four-Year Colleges." Inside Higher Ed, 29 Mar. 2016, www.insidehighered.com/news/2016/03/29/survey-finds-grade-inflation-continues-rise-four-year-colleges-not-community-college.

9   Deresiewicz, William. Excellent Sheep: The Miseducation of the American Elite and the Way to a Meaningful Life. Reprint, Free Press, 2015.

10 Millerd, Paul. "A Brief and Fun History Of The Strategy Consulting Industry 1900 - 2020." StrategyU, 31 July 2020, strategyu.co/strategy-consulting-history.

11 "The Big Law Trap - Guest Post by Ranjit Saimbi." Boundless: Beyond the Default Path, 23 July 2021, think-boundless.com/the-big-law-trap.

12   Graham, Paul. "How to Do What You Love." 2006. http://www.paulgraham.com/l ove.html

13   Watts, Alan. The Wisdom of Insecurity. Pantheon, 2021.

14   Lewis, C.S. "The Inner Ring," Memorial Lecture at King's College, University of London, in 1944, C.S. Lewis Society of California, 10 September 2021 https://ww w.lewissociety.org/innerring/

15   Taggart, Andrew. "A Modern Workforce Needs a New Take on Careers." Quartz, 27 July 2018, qz.com/work/1342191/a-modern-workforce-needs-a-new-take-on-careers.

16   Taggart, Andrew. "How Does the Desire for Wisdom Emerge?" Andrew James Taggart, Practical Philosopher, Ph.D., 4 June 2021, https://andrewjtaggart.com/20 21/06/05/how-does-the-desire-for-wisdom-emerge/.

17   Tedeschi, Richard G., and Lawrence G. Calhoun. "Posttraumatic Growth: Conceptual Foundations and Empirical Evidence." Psychological Inquiry, Vol. 15, No. 1, 2004, pp. 1–18. Crossref, doi:10.1207/s15327965pli1501_01.

WORK, WORK, WORK

18   Weber, Max, et al. The Protestant Ethic and the Spirit of Capitalism (Economy Editions). Dover Publications, 2003.

19   The Nichomachean Ethics of Aristotle, trans. F.H. Peters, M.A. 5th edition (London: Kegan Paul, Trench, Truebner & Co., 1893).

20   "2 Thessalonians 3." Holy Bible, New International Version. Bible Gateway, Biblica, Inc., 2011, www.biblegateway.com/passage/?search=2%20Thessalonians+3&version=NIV.

21   Weber, Max, et al. The Protestant Ethic and the Spirit of Capitalism (Economy Editions). Dover Publications, 2003.

22   Weber, Max, et al. The Protestant Ethic and the Spirit of Capitalism (Economy Editions). Dover Publications, 2003.

23   Fromm, Erich. Escape from Freedom. 13th Printing, Discus/Avon, 1972.

24   Vaynerchuk, Gary. Crush It!: Why NOW Is the Time to Cash In on Your Passion. First Edition, 1st Printing, Harper Studio, 2009.

25   Winfrey, Oprah. What I Know for Sure. First Edition; First Printing, Flatiron Books, 2014.

26   Petersen, Anne Helen. "How Millennials Became the Burnout Generation." BuzzFeed News, 2 Aug. 2020, www.buzzfeednews.com/article/annehelenpetersen/millennials-burnout-generation-debt-work.

27   Chetty, et al. "The Fading American Dream: Trends in Absolute Income Mobility Since 1940." Science 356(6336): 398-406, 2017. Figure 1B. Data downloaded from www.equality-of-opportunity.org/data/

28   Steinbeck, John, et al. America and Americans and Selected Nonfiction (Penguin Classics). Reissue, Penguin Classics, 2003.

29   Thiel, Peter with Blake Masters. Zero to One. Random House, 2014.

30   O'Shaughnessy, Jim. "Josh Wolfe – Inventing the Future." Infinite Loops Podcast, Apple Podcasts, 25 Mar. 2021, podcasts.apple.com/us/podcast/josh-wolfe-inventing-the-future-ep-40/id1489171190?i=1000514347427.

31   Thiel, Peter with Blake Masters. Zero to One. Random House, 2014.

32   Wrzesniewski, Amy, et. al., Jobs, Careers, and Callings: People's Relations to Their Work, Journal of Research in Personality, Vol. 31, Issue 1, 1997: 21-33.

33   Lashinsky, Adam. "100 Best Companies to Work For" Fortune, 10 Jan 2007.

34   2019 Staples Workplace Survey, https://www.staples.com/sbd/cre/marketing/workplace-survey/

35   Millerd, Paul.   "100+ Examples of Culture PR." Twitter, 28 Jan 2021.   twitter.com/p_millerd/status/1354773720795996161?s=20.

36   Bailey, C. and Adrian Madden. "What makes work meaningful - or meaningless?" MIT Sloan Management Review 57 (2016): 53-61.

37   Gorz, André. Reclaiming Work: Beyond the Wage-Based Society. 1st ed., Polity, 1999.

38   "2020 Annual Averages - Persons at Work in Agriculture and Nonagricultural Industries by Hours of Work." Bureau of Labor Statistics, 22 Jan. 2021, www.bls.gov-/cps/cpsaat19.htm.

39   Steelman, Aaron. "Employment Act of 1946." Federal Reserve History, 22 Nov. 2013, www.federalreservehistory.org/essays/employment-act-of-1946.

40   "Mr. Obama Goes to Washington." The Nation, 29 June 2015, www.thenation.com/article/archive/mr-obama-goes-washington.

41   Boyce, C. J., Wood, A. M., Daly, M., & Sedikides, C. (2015). Personality change following unemployment. Journal of Applied Psychology, 100(4), 991–1011. https://doi.org/10.1037/a0038647

42   Taniguchi, Hiromi. "Men's and Women's Volunteering: Gender Differences in the Effects of Employment and Family Characteristics." Nonprofit and Voluntary Sector Quarterly, Vol. 35, No. 1, Mar. 2006, pp. 83–101, doi:10.1177/0899764005282481.

43   Katz, L. F., & Krueger, A. B. (2018). The Rise and Nature of Alternative Work Arrangements in the United States, 1995–2015. ILR Review, 001979391882000. doi:10.1177/0019793918820008

44   Manyika, James, et al. "Independent Work: Choice, Necessity, and the Gig Economy." McKinsey & Company, 21 May 2019, www.mckinsey.com/featured-insights/employment-and-growth/independent-work-choice-necessity-and-the-gig-economy.

AWAKENING

45   "This Is What a Male Identity Crisis Sounds Like." ZigZag Podcast, 18 July 2019, podcasts.apple.com/us/podcast/this-is-what-a-male-identity-crisis-sounds-like/id1385700943?i=1000444766564.

46   Good Life Project, Austin Kleon, "Life on Creativity"

47   Vassallo, Daniel. "Only Intrinsic Motivation Lasts." Daniel Vassallo, 5 Oct. 2019, danielvassallo.com/only-intrinsic-motivation-lasts.

48   Leonard, George. Mastery. First Printing, Plume, 1992.

49   Reilly, William John. How to Avoid Work, By William J. Reilly. Harper & Bros, 1949.

50   "Who Decides How Much a Life Is Worth? (Ep. 344)." Freakonomics, 25 Nov. 2019, freakonomics.com/podcast/kenneth-feinberg.

BREAKING FREE

51   Boys, Bowery. "Ada Louise Huxtable, Still Shaping the New York Skyline." The Bowery Boys: New York City History, 14 Mar. 2021, www.boweryboyshistory.com/2021/03/ada-louise-huxtable-still-shaping.html.

52   Freudenberger, H. J. (1974). Staff Burn-Out. Journal of Social Issues, 30(1), 159–165. doi:10.1111/j.1540-4560.1974.tb00706.x

53   Freudenberger, Herbert J. (1989) Burnout, Loss, Grief & Care, 3:1-2, 1-10.

54   InformedHealth.org [Internet]. Cologne, Germany: Institute for Quality and Efficiency in Health Care (IQWiG); 2006-. Depression: What is burnout? [Updated 2020 Jun 18]. Available from: https://www.ncbi.nlm.nih.gov/books/NBK279286/

55   Freudenberger, H. J. (1974). Staff Burn-Out. Journal of Social Issues, 30(1), 159–165. doi:10.1111/j.1540-4560.1974.tb00706.x

56   Pieper, Josef, et al. Leisure, The Basis Of Culture. 1st ed., St. Augustine's Press, 1998.

57   Pieper, Josef, et al. Leisure, The Basis Of Culture. 1st ed., St. Augustine's Press, 1998.

58 Taggart, Andrew. "If Work Dominated Your Every Moment Would Life Be Worth Living? | Aeon Ideas." Aeon, 20 Dec. 2016, aeon.co/ideas/if-work-dominated-your-every-moment-would-life-be-worth-living.

59 Zuzunaga, Andrés. "COSMOGRAMA - Escuela de Astrología en Barcelona y Online." COSMOGRAMA, www.cosmograma.com/proposito.php. Accessed 7 Jan. 2022.

60 Winn, Marc. "What Is Your Ikigai? · The View Inside Me." The View Inside Me, theviewinside.me/what-is-your-ikigai. Accessed 7 Jan. 2022.

61 Kowalski, Kyle. "The True Meaning of Ikigai: Definitions, Diagrams & Myths about the Japanese Life Purpose." Sloww, 29 Dec. 2020, www.sloww.co/ikigai.

62 Erich Fromm: The Art of Loving: The Centennial Edition (Hardcover); 2000 Edition. Erich Fromm, 1672.

THE FIRST STEPS

63 "What Living on a Boat for 18 Months Can Teach You about Work & Life (John Zeratsky)." Reimagine Work Podcast, uploaded by Reimagine Work, 12 June 2019, podcasts.apple.com/us/podcast/what-living-on-a-boat-for-18-months-can-teach-you/id1328600107?i=1000441298765.

64 "Imagining A New American Dream (Diania Merriam, Econome Conference)." Reimagine Work Podcast, 8 Jan. 2020, podcasts.apple.com/us/podcast/imagining-new-american-dream-diania-merriam-econome/id1328600107?i=1000461954819.

65 "What Happens Six Months (and Three Months) before You Quit? - Michael Ashcroft." Reimagine Work Podcast, 13 Apr. 2021, podcasts.apple.com/us/podcast/what-happens-six-months-and-three-months-before-you/id1328600107?i=1000516993222.

66 "How Your Earliest Journeys Transform You." Rolf Potts, Deviate Podcast, 14 July 2021, rolfpotts.com/podcast/vagabonding-audio-companion-2.

67 Davidai, S., & Gilovich, T. (2018). The ideal road not taken: The self-discrepancies involved in people's most enduring regrets. Emotion, 18(3), 439–452. https://doi.org/10.1037/emo0000326

68 Ferriss, Tim. "The Tim Ferriss Show Transcripts: Gretchen Rubin (#290)." The Blog of Author Tim Ferriss, 16 Jan. 2020, tim.blog/2018/02/04/the-tim-ferriss-show-transcripts-gretchen-rubin.

69 Callard, Agnes. Aspiration: The Agency of Becoming. Reprint, Oxford University Press, 2019.

70 Callard, Agnes. Aspiration: The Agency of Becoming. Reprint, Oxford University Press, 2019.

71 Callard, Agnes. Aspiration: The Agency of Becoming. Reprint, Oxford University Press, 2019.

72 "Chris Donohoe on Quitting the Corporate World & Founding His Own Firm." Boundless: Beyond The Default Path, 19 June 2019, think-boundless.com/boundless-podcast-episode-4-chris-donohoe-on-jumping-into-a-world-of-limitless-creation.

73 "Screw The Cubicle With A Side Of Pineapple (Lydia Lee)." Boundless: Beyond The Default Path, 9 Feb. 2019, think-boundless.com/screw-the-cubicle-lydia-lee.

74 Ferriss, Tim. "Fear-Setting: The Most Valuable Exercise I Do Every Month." The Blog of Author Tim Ferriss, 15 Nov. 2020, tim.blog/2017/05/15/fear-setting.

75 Burnett, Bill, and Dave Evans. Designing Your Life: How to Build a Well-Lived, Joyful Life. Illustrated, Knopf, 2016.

76 McMillen, Amy. Reclaiming Control: Looking Inward to Recalibrate Your Life. New Degree Press, 2020.

WISDOM OF THE PATHLESS PATH

77 Solnit, Rebecca. A Field Guide to Getting Lost. Reprint, Penguin Books, 2006.

78 Tzu, Lao, and Stephen Mitchell. Tao Te Ching: A New English Version (Perennial Classics). Reprint, Harper Perennial Modern Classics, 2006.

79 "John Steinbeck's Letter of Fatherly Advice to His Son." Penguin, 7 Apr. 2020, www.penguin.co.uk/articles/2015/read-john-steinbeck-s-letter-of-fatherly-advice-to-his-son.html.

80 Campbell, Joseph, and Diane Osbon. Reflections on the Art of Living: A Joseph Campbell Companion. Reprint, Harper Perennial, 1995.

81 Satyanand, Mohit. "I Quit Working Full-Time Years Ago—Here's Why I Recommend It Highly." Quartz India, 20 May 2015, qz.com/india/241043/i-quit-working-full-time-years-ago-heres-why-i-recommend-it-highly.

82 Quote provided in private conversation, November 2021

83 "Jacqueline Jensen on Sabbaticals, Rethinking Work and Building a 'Calm Company.'" Apple Podcasts, 26 Sept. 2018, podcasts.apple.com/us/podcast/jacqueline-jensen-on-sabbaticals-rethinking-work-building/id1328600107?i=1000420486588.

84 Edward. "The Eureka Heuristic and The Mini Retirement." Edward Says, 28 Apr. 2021, edwardsays.com/the-eureka-heuristic-and-the-extended-break.

85 Rachitsky, Lenny. "On Taking Time Off." Lenny's Newsletter, 20 Apr. 2021, www.lennysnewsletter.com/p/sabbatical-time-off.

86   Anthony, Andrew. "Why the Secret to Productivity Isn't Longer Hours." The Guardian, 22 Mar. 2018, www.theguardian.com/money/2017/jan/22/alex-soojung-kim-pang-interview-rest-why-you-get-more-done-when-you-work-less.

87   Institute for Social Research, University of Michigan. "Aging in the 21St Century: Challenges and Opportunities for Americans." Health and Retirement Study, 2017, hrs.isr.umich.edu/publications.

88   Ferriss, Timothy. The 4-Hour Workweek: Escape 9–5, Live Anywhere, and Join the New Rich. Expanded, Updated ed., Harmony, 2009.

89   Ferriss, Timothy. The 4-Hour Workweek: Escape 9–5, Live Anywhere, and Join the New Rich. Expanded, Updated ed., Harmony, 2009.

90   Rao, Venkatesh. "Personal Futurism for Indies." The Art of Gig, 19 Mar. 2021, artofgig.substack.com/p/personal-futurism-for-indies.

91   Mill, John S. On Liberty. London: John W. Parker and Son, West Strand, 1859.

92   Mill, John S. On Liberty. London: John W. Parker and Son, West Strand, 1859.

93   McCabe, Sean. "Origin of Seventh Week Sabbaticals." *Sabbatical.Blog*, 14 Aug. 2018, sabbatical.blog/2018/08/origin-of-seventh-week-sabbaticals.

94   Whyte, William, and Joseph Nocera. The Organization Man. Revised ed., University of Pennsylvania Press, 2002.

95   Whyte, William, and Joseph Nocera. The Organization Man. Revised ed., University of Pennsylvania Press, 2002.

96   Bevan, Thomas. "The Misery Tax." The Commonplace, 20 Sept. 2020, thomasjbevan.substack.com/p/the-misery-tax.

97   Robin, Vicki, et al. Your Money or Your Life. Revised, Penguin Books, 2008.

98   "Quitting To Teach History to 500k+ on TikTok" Reimagine Work Podcast, 11 Jan. 2021, podcasts.apple.com/us/podcast/quitting-to-teach-history-to-500k-on-tiktok-michael/id1328600107?i=1000504969548.

99   Salzberg, Sharon. Faith: Trusting Your Own Deepest Experience. Reissue, Riverhead Books, 2003.

REDEFINE SUCCESS

100   Success Index, Gallup, 2019 (https://news.gallup.com/opinion/gallup/266927/americans-perceptions-success.aspx)

101   Alexander, Scott. "Book Review: The Secret Of Our Success." Slate Star Codex, 31 Dec. 2020, slatestarcodex.com/2019/06/04/book-review-the-secret-of-our-success.

102 Lowe, Zach. "Why the Collapse of the Warriors Feels so Abrupt." ABC7 San Francisco, 2 July 2019, abc7news.com/sports/why-the-collapse-of-the-warriors-feels-so-abrupt/5374773.

103 Holiday, Ryan. "34 Mistakes on the Way to 34 Years Old." RyanHoliday.Net, 16 June 2021, ryanholiday.net/34-mistakes-on-the-way-to-34-years-old.

104 Shilton, A. "You Accomplished Something Great. So Now What?" The New York Times, 2 June 2019, www.nytimes.com/2019/05/28/smarter-living/you-accomplished-something-great-so-now-what.html

105 Roosevelt, Eleanor. You Learn by Living: Eleven Keys for a More Fulfilling Life. 50th Anniversary ed., Harper Perennial Modern Classics, 2011.

106 Thoreau, Henry David. Walden. Project Gutenberg, 1995.

107 Smith, Adam. The Theory of Moral Sentiments.

108 "Social Status: Down the Rabbit Hole | Melting Asphalt." Melting Asphalt, 2015, meltingasphalt.com/social-status-down-the-rabbit-hole.

109 Kendzior, Sarah. "The Perils of the Prestige Economy." Sarah Kendzior, 16 June 2013, sarahkendzior.com/2013/06/16/the-perils-of-the-prestige-economy.

110 Graham, Paul. "The Lesson to Unlearn." Paul Graham's Website, www.paulgraham.com/lesson.html?viewfullsite=1. Accessed 7 Jan. 2022.

111 "The Lesson to Unlearn." Paul Graham: Essays, 2020, paulgraham.com/lesson.html.

112 "The Lesson to Unlearn." Paul Graham: Essays, 2020, paulgraham.com/lesson.html.

113 "'People like Us Do Things like This.'" Seth's Blog, 17 Dec. 2020, seths.blog/2013/07/peoplelike-us-do-stuff-like-this.

114 Scott, James. Seeing like a State: How Certain Schemes to Improve the Human Condition Have Failed. 0 ed., Yale University Press, 1999

115 Millerd, Paul. "Ben Hunt on Industrially Necessary Paths & How To Live In The Now." Boundless: Beyond The Default Path, 25 Sept. 2021, think-boundless.com/ben-hunt.

116 "Narratives, Work & What Matters - Ben Hunt." Reimagine Work Podcast, 6 July 2021, podcasts.apple.com/gb/podcast/narratives-work-what-matters-ben-hunt/id1328600107?i=1000527989137.

117 Marlar, By Jenny. "Global Payroll to Population Rate Drops to 26% in 2012." Gallup.Com, 7 May 2021, news.gallup.com/poll/163841/global-payroll-population-rate-drops-2012.aspx.

118 "S4 EP10: This Is What a Male Identity Crisis Sounds Like" ZigZag Podcast, 18 July 2019, zigzagpod.com.

119 "The Formless Path - Money, Fatherhood & Creativity (Howard Gray)." Reimagine Work Podcast, 27 Sept. 2021, https://think-boundless.com/podcast.

120 USA Today. "No Opening Day: Ex-Major Leaguers Struggle with Retirement." AP, 26 Mar. 2018, eu.usatoday.com/story/sports/mlb/2018/03/26/no-opening-day-ex-major-leaguers-struggle-with-retirement/33286277.

121 Turner, Broderick. "Former Players Say Kobe Bryant Must Work on Transition Game." Baltimore Sun, 6 Dec. 2015, www.baltimoresun.com/la-sp-nba-players-retiring-20151206-story.html.

122 Solnit, Rebecca. A Field Guide to Getting Lost. Reprint, Penguin Books, 2006.

123 Thoreau, Henry David. Walden. Project Gutenberg, 1995, www.gutenberg.org/-files/205/205-h/205-h.htm.

124 Jarvis, Paul. Company of One: Why Staying Small Is the Next Big Thing for Business. Reprint, Mariner Books, 2020.

125 Jarvis, Paul. "Enough." Fathom Analytics, 2018, usefathom.com/blog/enough.

126 Glei, Jocelyn. "Check Yourself Before You Wreck Yourself •." Jocelyn K. Glei, 12 July 2017, jkglei.com/burnout.

127 Thompson, Derek. "The New Economics of Happiness." *The Atlantic*, 23 May 2012, www.theatlantic.com/business/archive/2012/05/the-new-economics-of-happiness/257557.

128 "The Science of Scarcity." Harvard Magazine, 16 Nov. 2020, www.harvard-magazine.com/2015/05/the-science-of-scarcity.

129 Becker, Ernest. The Denial of Death First Edition 1973. Generic, 1973.

THE REAL WORK OF YOUR LIFE

130 "A Larger Language for Business." *Harvard Business Review*, 1 Aug. 2014, hbr.org/2007/05/a-larger-language-for-business.

131 "David Whyte — The Conversational Nature of Reality." The On Being Project, 1 July 2020, onbeing.org/programs/david-whyte-the-conversational-nature-of-reality.

132 Deresiewicz, William. "Solitude and Leadership." The American Scholar, 28 May 2019, theamericanscholar.org/solitude-and-leadership.

133 "John O'Nolan on Life as a Nomad, Ghost and Optimising for Happiness." Not Over-thinking Podcast, 17 Nov. 2020, podcasts.apple.com/sg/podcast/john-onolan-on-life-as-nomad-ghost-optimising-for-happiness/id1456538451?i=1000499021785.

134 Cope, Stephen. The Great Work of Your Life: A Guide for the Journey to Your True Calling. Reprint, Bantam, 2015.

135 Cope, Stephen. The Great Work of Your Life: A Guide for the Journey to Your True Calling. Reprint, Bantam, 2015.

136 Thoreau, Henry David. The Writings of Henry David Thoreau, Volume VII (of 20) Journal I, 1837–1846. Project Gutenberg, 2018.

137 Kegan, Robert. In Over Our Heads. Amsterdam, Netherlands, Amsterdam University Press, 1994.

138 Brown, Brené. "Shame v. Guilt - Brené Brown." Brené Brown Personal Website, 21 Aug. 2019, brenebrown.com/blog/2013/01/14/shame-v-guilt/#close-popup.

139 Brown, Brené. "Shame v. Guilt - Brené Brown." Brené Brown Personal Website, 21 Aug. 2019, brenebrown.com/blog/2013/01/14/shame-v-guilt/#close-popup.

140 Junger, Sebastian. Tribe: On Homecoming and Belonging. 1st ed., Twelve, 2016.

141 Miller, Jonny. Remember, Forget, Remember, 2021.

142 Godin, Seth. Linchpin: Are You Indispensable? 1st ed., Portfolio, 2011.

143 Clip from The Moment With Brian Koppelman, Episode: "Seth Godin 9/17/19" https://www.listennotes.com/clips/new-seth-godin-91719-OX9ZDTLFl8K/

144 Cowen, Tyler. "The High-Return Activity of Raising Others' Aspirations." Marginal REVOLUTION, 21 Oct. 2018, marginalrevolution.com/marginal-revolution/2018/10/high-return-activity-raising-others-aspirations.html.

145 "Wells Fargo | Violation Tracker." © Good Jobs First, 2021, violationtracker.goodjobsfirst.org/parent/wells-fargo.

146 "What Was the Hardest Thing You Went through in Life, and How Did You Get Past It?", 2016, www.quora.com/What-was-the-hardest-thing-you-went-through-in-life-and-how-did-you-get-past-it.

147 "Mapping Meaning in a Digital Age | Maria Popova." The On Being Project, 2 July 2020, onbeing.org/programs/mapping-meaning-digital-age-maria-popova.

148 Zinsser, William. On Writing Well: The Classic Guide to Writing Nonfiction. 30th Anniversary ed., Harper Perennial, 2016.

149 Russell, Bertrand. In Praise of Idleness and Other Essays. W.W. NORTON & Co., 2021.

150 Russell, Bertrand. In Praise of Idleness and Other Essays. W.W. NORTON & Co., 2021.

PLAYING THE LONG GAME

151 Street, Farnam. "Inversion: The Power of Avoiding Stupidity." Farnam Street, 25 Jan. 2020, fs.blog/inversion.

152 Carse, James, et al. Finite and Infinite Games. Simon and Schuster Audio, 2018.

153 Fromm, Erich. Escape from Freedom. 1st Edition, Holt Paperbacks, 1994.

154 Fromm, Erich. Escape from Freedom. 1st Edition, Holt Paperbacks, 1994.

155 Fromm, Erich. Escape from Freedom. 1st Edition, Holt Paperbacks, 1994.

156 Wallace, David Foster. This Is Water: Some Thoughts, Delivered on a Significant Occasion, about Living a Compassionate Life. 1st ed., Little, Brown and Company, 2009.

157 Fromm, Erich. The Art of Loving. Harper Perennial Modern Classics, 2006.

158 Sarris, Simon. "The Most Precious Resource Is Agency." By Simon Sarris - The Map Is Mostly Water, 1 July 2021, simonsarris.substack.com/p/the-most-precious-resource-is-agency.

159 Fromm, Erich. Escape from Freedom. 1st Edition, Holt Paperbacks, 1994.

160 Parton, Dolly. Twitter, 8 Apr. 2015, twitter.com/DollyParton/

161 Quoidbach, Jordi, et al. "The End of History Illusion." Science, vol. 339, no. 6115, 2013, pp. 96–98. Crossref, doi:10.1126/science.1229294.

162 Harari, Yuval Noah. 21 Lessons for the 21st Century. Reprint, Random House, 2019.

163 Thompson, E. P. "TIME, WORK-DISCIPLINE, AND INDUSTRIAL CAPI-TALISM." Past and Present, vol. 38, no. 1, 1967, pp. 56–97. Crossref, doi:10.1093/past/38.1.56.

164 Berry, Wendell. The Unsettling of America: Culture & Agriculture. Reprint, Counterpoint, 2015.

165 Eisenstein, Charles. Sacred Economics: Money, Gift, and Society in the Age of Transition. North Atlantic Books, 2011.

166 Wu, Tim. "Opinion | The Tyranny of Convenience." The New York Times, 16 Feb. 2018, www.nytimes.com/2018/02/16/opinion/sunday/tyranny-convenience.html.

167 "Gift Economy." Andrew James Taggart, Practical Philosopher, Ph.D., 29 Nov. 2020, andrewjtaggart.com/gift-economy.

168 "Sacred Economics: Money, the Gift, and Society in the Age of Transition." Charles Eisenstein's Personal Site, 2012. charleseisenstein.org/essays/sacred-economics-money-the-gift-and-society-in-the-age-of-transition.

169 Godin, Seth. Linchpin: Are You Indispensable? 1st ed., Portfolio, 2011.

170 "Sacred Economics: Money, the Gift, and Society in the Age of Transition." Charles Eisenstein's Personal Site, 2012.

171 Albom, Mitch, *Tuesdays With Morrie, 1995*

172 Albom, Mitch, *Tuesdays With Morrie, 1995*

173 Albom, Mitch, *Tuesdays With Morrie, 1995*

174 Albom, Mitch, *Tuesdays With Morrie, 1995*

175 Albom, Mitch, *Tuesdays With Morrie, 1995*

176 Live, Washington Post. "Transcript: The Optimist: A Conversation with Mitch Albom." Washington Post, 26 May 2021, www.washingtonpost.com/washington-post-live/2021/05/26/transcript-optimist-conversation-with-mitch-albom.

177 Solnit, Rebecca. A Field Guide to Getting Lost. Reprint, Penguin Books, 2006.

178 "Hunter S. Thompson's Letter on Finding Your Purpose and Living a Meaningful Life." Farnam Street, 10 Nov. 2019, fs.blog/2014/05/hunter-s-thompson-to-hume-logan.

179 Oliver, Mary. "The Summer Day." *The Library of Congress*, www.loc.gov/programs/poetry-and-literature/poet-laureate/poet-laureate-projects/poetry-180/all-poems/item/poetry-180-133/the-summer-day. Accessed 12 Jan. 2022.

About the Author

Paul Millerd is an independent writer, freelancer, coach, and digital creator. He has written online for many years and has built a growing audience of curious humans from around the world. He spent several years working in strategy consulting before deciding to walk away and embrace a pathless path. He is fascinated about how our relationship to work is shifting and how more people can live lives where they can thrive.

You can connect with me on:
🌐 https://www.think-boundless.com
🐦 https://twitter.com/p_millerd

Subscribe to my newsletter:
✉️ https://think-boundless.com/subscribe

Photo Credit: Alicia Tsai - https://www.aliciatsai.photography/

9 798985 515329